# from DARKNESS to LIGHT

# from DARKNESS to LIGHT

Jeff Harshbarger
with Liz Harshbarger

How to rescue
someone you love
from the occult

**Bridge-Logos**
Gainesville, Florida 32614

Bridge-Logos
Gainesville, FL 32614 USA

04          1

Library of Congress Catalog Card Number: pending
International Standard Book Number 0-88270-912-7

This book is dedicated to
Harry and Jo Richardson

*For He has rescued us from the dominion of darkness
and brought us into the kingdom of the
Son He loves (Colossians 1:13).*

# Contents

## Part One: Jeff's story

## Part Two: Quick study of the occult

# Part Three: How to rescue someone you love from the occult

# FOREWORD

My name is Jeff Harshbarger. I'm a former Satanist who was literally wrenched from the death grip of the devil by Jesus Christ, who foiled my suicide not once, but twice because He loved me too much to let me die, and moreover, had plans for my life. For the past twenty years, I've devoted my life to reaching back into the darkness to rescue other people from the occult. My wife Liz and I operate Refuge Ministries, and work 24 hours a day, 7 days a week on a mission to take back the precious souls that Satan has claimed as his, and help return them to the tender, forgiving, loving, protecting arms of God.

You've picked up this book because someone you love is mired in the occult, and you want to rescue and lead him or her back to the Lord. Perhaps you're not even sure that you're dealing with the occult, and you need some education and confirmation. Perhaps you're not sure about what to do in order to step in and rescue. Perhaps you're afraid that you're not sufficient or strong enough to battle Satan for a soul ... and win. This book is for you. Together, we'll explore the occult, and then I'll tell you what to do. I'm with you.

This book is written for you in three parts. The first is my story. I use my own life—ordinary in every way—to demonstrate how easily despair and emptiness can set in on a child, how effortlessly evil moves in to fill the gap, how logically a life can be absorbed into the dark side, and how lovingly and dramatically God steps in to rescue. As I tell my story, I hope you'll be struck by innocence, gullibility, and ordinariness of my being drawn into Satanism. You'll clearly understand the dangerous progression from curiosity and experimentation into full-blown commitment to the demonic. And I trust that you'll be filled with hope and joy when you read about lengths to which God will go to reclaim a lamb who's strayed.

In the second part of the book, we'll turn the story from mine to yours. I'll teach you the basics of the occult practices, and show you some of the clues (symbols and behaviors) that let you know which practice your loved one has chosen. I'll even show you how the occult has quietly infiltrated our culture so that very few people pay attention to creeping evil … until it's too late.

In the third part of the book, I'll teach you what to do: first, how to protect yourself before you battle the forces of darkness, and then, how to rescue your loved one. Together we can do it.

At the end of this book, I've given you a way to contact us directly. Liz and I stand by to help you. Together with God, we stand with you against Satan. We'll bring your beloved home.

Part One

Jeff's story

# Chapter One

**I WANTED TO DIE.**

I had made the decision. It was the only option left.

As I paced in my bedroom, I could hear the members of my Satanic coven at the other end of the house. Laughing, probably a little high. So confident in what we had taught them. "Confident." I smiled weakly to myself, everything that I had put my hope and heart into had failed me. I thought that I knew, I thought that being the ultimate servant of "almighty Satan" would bring what I had searched for all of my life. But no. I was being tormented by the absence of meaning and purpose. Tormented by the fact that I had received no answers to the many questions that I had. Tormented by the knowledge that my greatest enemy evidently had the power to interfere with my quest for darkness.

I looked down at the diamond on my hand and smiled again. Death would come easily. I would be the ultimate sacrifice to my god, and in dying by my own hand, I would show this Jesus that he had no power over me. "F___ you!" I said through my teeth toward the ceiling. "I hate you! You're not going to stop me!"

With resolve, I quickly walked out of my bedroom through the living room of partying young Satanists, and out into the cool October sun. Purchasing the gun had been easy. I told the pawnshop owner that my home had been broken into. He wished me luck with a smile. Manipulating people was my specialty. I enjoyed how weak and simpleminded people seemed to be.

It was early evening as I left the pawnshop and walked through the back streets of Muncie, Indiana toward the nearest hotel. I shuffled through golden leaves that had already fallen. "This will be my last autumn," I thought, almost relieved. I pushed to the back of my mind memories of a time when I loved the crisp aroma of fall. I shoved aside memories of autumn football with friends, and thoughts of the kind of family that I had always wanted.

**❝My mother would know by tomorrow. Her prayers had failed.❞**

Choosing the rear entrance into the parking lot of the Holiday Inn, I stashed the gun, marijuana, and whisky behind a bush, went into the lobby, and booked a room. When the unsuspecting clerk put the key into my hand, I returned to my hiding place, retrieved my belongings, and slipped quietly down the hall and into my room. I tossed the gun on the bed and sat myself down next to it. Pulling out my brown paper sack, I lit a joint. The smoke began to circle my head and I could feel myself starting to relax. But I didn't want to just relax; I wanted to be numb. I opened the bottle of Jack Daniels and took a swig, coughing as the liquor burned its way down my throat. Good. I could feel confidence in what I was about to do growing. Well, this was the end, here in this hotel. I would probably make the evening news. My mother would know by tomorrow. Her prayers had failed.

I loaded the gun and put the barrel to my head. A wave of fear came to me that I hadn't expected. "I'm not afraid to die!" I scoffed. I grew still at the sound of my own words. I put the barrel to my head again, closed my eyes, drew a deep breath—and *fear* again. I heard words resounding in my head, "Where are you going to spend eternity?"

Sweat beaded on my forehead head and my hands shook. I couldn't pull the trigger. Suddenly, I was exhausted, completely spent. I relaxed onto the bed and fell into a fitful sleep. I woke up the next morning, grabbed my gun, and left the hotel. Walking home, I felt the failure of my life, failure even in my death.

I arrived home knowing what I had done and what I had failed to do. I could feel the anger welling up inside of me. Today. Today my attempt to destroy myself would succeed. That afternoon, after making sure that no one knew what I was up to, I found a thick rope in the garage and made a strong noose. I tied the other end securely around the rafter. I wasn't even

**❝I loaded the gun and put the barrel to my head.❞**

going to allow myself to think this time. I stood on a chair and slipped the noose around my neck. Rough cords bit my skin as I tightened it. I quickly kicked the chair out from under me with a brief thrill of excitement in finally succeeding and facing the master that I had served so faithfully. I felt the rope tighten and my body jerk, and then before I knew what had happened, the noose slipped over my head and I hit the hard cement floor. Gasping to regain my breath, I couldn't believe that I was still alive. Why was I not dead!?! How could I have failed again!?!

Depression flooded over me. Twice I had tried to end my miserable existence; twice I had failed. I dragged my aching body off the floor and went into the house. Now what? Was there a way out? I didn't know. What about the questions that were still rolling around in my head. Even my "great" mentor had been lacking an answer.

The rest of my coven had all arrived home and were starting their nightly tradition of partying themselves into oblivion. Automatically I grabbed one of the cold beers that were in the fridge. I put it to my lips and attempted to take a big gulp, but the smell repulsed me! I spit the mouthful onto the floor. "This is stupid!" I thought. "I've been drinking for years!" I grabbed another one, and couldn't even try. The smell made my stomach heave. Glaring at the coven members around me, I threw the second one in the sink and fished in my pocket for a joint. But the smell of it also made me ill. I lit a cigarette and took a deep drag. My lips and throat seared in pain.

My mood darkened. Members of my coven, deciding that I was no longer fun to be around, took the party elsewhere. I stood alone in the house as they pulled out of the driveway.

I went outside to clear the confusion from my head. My good friend's alcohol and drugs now made me sick to my stomach. I couldn't die! S__t! I couldn't even smoke! The weight of my life made my body feel heavy. With no other way of escape, I walked back into the house and lay down on my bed. If I could just sleep, I could relieve my pain.

I fell on my bed and lay on my back, staring at the ceiling. With a sigh that came from the depths of my being, I closed my eyes. From the pit of my stomach came a sob. Without being able to control myself, I began to cry.

Years of seeking answers had produced nothing. Everything that I had touched had failed. I just wanted to die and had failed at even that. Failure. All I felt was failure.

There was a tremendous relief in my tears. I continued to weep for several more minutes. From the quiet of the house came a voice, strong and clear.

"Get out," it said.

I stopped crying immediately. The voice had come from the foot of my bed. Looking in that direction, I saw no one. I grew tense and lay very still. Perhaps this demon had come to punish my failure. The thought made me shudder.

Again, the voice insisted, "Get out!"

This time I heard the voice from right beside my face. I could almost feel the breath on my skin. This was no demon. Out! I must get out! Without hesitating, I went to the nearest porthole of escape. I threw open the window beside my bed and slid to the ground just below.

The night was cold and clear. I turned away from the house and walked into a presence that was unfamiliar to

**❝At that moment, I felt overwhelming love and compassion.❞**

me. Yet, somehow I knew it. This being was more powerful than anyone or anything, any person or any demon that I had met in all my years as a Satanist. At that moment, I felt overwhelming love and compassion. I began to tremble all over, falling willingly to my face. This was what I had been seeking. Ultimate power. This was who I was looking for. Unfathomable forgiveness and love. I was in the presence of God. The God of my enemies, the God of the Christians ... but God nonetheless.

Looking up through my tears into the dark and starry sky, I said, "Jesus, just make my life O.K."

I wasn't conscious of accepting Him as my Lord and Savior at that moment. I just needed to make it through that moment in my life. I thought that I would only ask Him to help me.

And He did.

# Chapter Two

**I WAS BORN IN CAMP LEJEUNNE**, North Carolina. I was the fourth child in a family of five children. My father, a striking, 6-foot tall man with black hair, was a respected Staff Sergeant in the United States Marine Corps. Although my father was a very caring man, it was his responsibility to prepare our boys for war. He was as tough as they come. Tough on his soldiers, tough on his children. After all, he was preparing us for the biggest war of all. Life.

Because of this, I had a very hard time bonding to my father. To begin with, he was a tough person. There were no second chances. One mistake, intentional or not, and we kids would suffer the consequences. I can remember at times being punished and not really understanding what I had done wrong. On top of this, he was gone a lot from home. But I loved him as much as a son could love his father. I longed to be closer, but I learned to be afraid of him.

My mother, on the other hand, overcompensated for my fathers' absence and rigidity. She was a petite brunette with an infectious smile. Mom could be overbearing at times because she was constantly running interference with my father. Usually they would end up fighting. My father wanted to make a man out of me;

my mother overprotected both my brother and me. We were, after all, just little boys.

Upon returning from the Vietnam War, my father began to drink heavily. Later in my life, I was told that he had been involved in an ambush and although he had been shot, was the only survivor. None of the young men under his charge made it. But discovering this tragic episode in my father's life and maybe even understanding his anger didn't make him easier to bear.

Our family didn't seem to have the good times that I saw other families having. We never laughed together, or enjoyed peaceful evenings. We were very quiet, mostly out of fear.

My father was hardly ever home, but when he was, my parents fought constantly. As time went on, the fighting intensified. We kids were scared a lot. How I wished my parents would just get along.

Around the age of five, the Marine Corps transferred my father to Camp Pendleton, and my family moved to California. I fell in love with California right away. Suddenly, everything was alive! The golden sunshine was wonderful. The air smelled of lemons and oranges. I tried to figure out what exactly an avocado was. There seemed to be no limit to the new discoveries waiting to be made. There was even a creek that ran behind our house. I used to love fishing for crawdaddies, wearing my cowboy boots and carrying my weapon of choice, a butter knife!

My parents seemed to get along better here. My dad came home daily after work and enjoyed working on our old Rambler in the driveway.

We became more mobile as a family. We actually went into town and shopped. We went out to eat and attempted to enjoy ourselves. My brother joined the Boys

Club, and both of us were given the freedom to venture to the candy store. We rode our bikes in the warm sunshine, just glad to be alive. Hope began to stir in my heart. Were we actually becoming a normal family?

I even did well in school, both academically and socially. The violence and instability of my earlier years had not affected me. It was smooth sailing in the sunny newfound wonderland. I loved being alive. It seemed to me that nothing could or would go wrong here. Whatever the problems were in North Carolina, they seemed to be distant memory that would soon fade altogether.

**"Unfortunately, there was soon trouble in Paradise."**

Unfortunately, there was soon trouble in Paradise. My parents informed us one evening that we were going to move again, this time to Indiana. I felt myself stiffen and fight back tears. "Why?" I thought, "Everything is great. No need to move. We are happy here! Where were on earth was Indiana? What was going to happen?" I didn't like the sounds of the thoughts as they began to fill my mind.

My dad had finished his career in the Marine Corps, and we were moving to Indiana to be closer to my mother's brother. My dad was sure he could find work there in order to provide for his family. As we packed our belongings onto the moving truck, and headed down the road, I wondered if this next move might be as good as the last one. We had gone from being in North Carolina with its fighting and violence to the bright sunshine and good life of California. What would Indiana bring to our family?

We headed cross-country in the Rambler toward the Midwest. Rather than dwell on grief and uncertainty, I tried to anticipate the adventure. Traveling through the Wild West toward an unknown place should be fun. My parents saw things differently. We were on a mission that would be accomplished only as we reached our destination. No time for breaks ... sight-seeing or any other kind. I watched out the window as we roared past one incredible place after another. Finally, to my great delight, we pulled into an Indian reservation. Our visit was brief, but at least we were able to get out of the car!

Before I knew it, we were back on the road. The beautiful desert scenery began to change to flat plains and farms. Where were the palm trees? No lemons? No oranges? "Please," I thought, "at least let there be a creek with crawdaddies." This place was beginning to look too much like North Carolina. I had a sickening feeling that life had just taken a turn for the worst.

Our new home was located in the small town of Upland, Indiana. We arrived midsummer so that there was some time to adjust to our new surroundings. There was no creek nearby, but there was a lake pretty close to our trailer court. This town was small enough for me to walk anywhere I needed to go. There was even a candy store nearby, just like California. Maybe the place wasn't so bad after all.

Unfortunately, my dad didn't adjust to his new life. It was difficult for him to go from being a respected Marine Sergeant to "just a civilian." It was harder still to find a good job. Soon, he began to drink heavily again. Shortly after that, the fighting resumed more intensely than before.

It was hard enough to adjust to life in a new place: new school, new people, with unfamiliar accents, and Indiana in the fall and winter. The adjustment was made nearly impossible, because life in our home was unstable and embattled. My stomach was starting to gnaw with pent-up frustration. I used to stare out the window at the frozen school yard and wish for sunny California where I felt so alive and my family was happy. Now all I could feel was sad. It felt as though a part of me had begun to die.

# Chapter Three

**THE FIRST YEAR IN INDIANA** remained in brutally sharp contrast to the fun of California. Instead of enjoying being together, our whole family was fighting. Instead of doing well academically and socially, my siblings and I were now failing and fearful. I had withdrawn and was having trouble making friends.

To make matters worse, my dad began to spend a great deal of his time at a bar downtown. Most nights, he came home drunk. In a town as small as this one was, people were bound to notice, and they did. We gained quite a reputation. The police got to know us very well because they were called to our house often by our neighbors. Even as a child, I felt the shame of being the son of the town's drunk.

By the end of the school year, my parents decided to move again. Things would be different in a town where no one knew us. We could make a fresh start. We moved to Marion, Indiana, where I would start the third grade. For a while, things did seem better. We moved into our first real house, away from the trailer parks we had known. My dad found a good job and was able to provide for us quite well. My parents got a new car, and we kids got bikes. I even liked the new school better than I had in Upland.

I started to hope again. But our situation was hopeless. It didn't take long before my father's drinking became even more severe. Worse, the fighting between my parents escalated into physical violence and fist fighting. I can still remember being startled out of my sleep by their screaming. Then my dad turned his drunken rage and violence toward us kids. Many nights I was afraid to fall asleep for fear that something bad would happen. For the first time in my life, I began to wish that he were dead.

I was no longer able to function in school. I just wanted to stay home and cry. When I did go to school, I sometimes broke down in class. This made me a target for other boys who were looking for someone to beat up. I remember sitting in a corner of the playground, just wanting to be left alone, when this big kid approached me. He mocked me and made fun of me for being a crybaby. Before I knew what was happening, I found myself beating the kid up. All of the years of pent-up frustration and anger made me a ferocious fighter. This kid was twice my size. Yet, I took him in no time. My reputation as a fighter gave me a newfound respect among my peers. I had a circle of friends who, like me, didn't have the best reputations. We didn't care. No one pushed us around. I now knew a little about having power, and even in the third grade, I liked it.

This new reputation soon caused the adults at my school to notice me. My teacher referred me to a counselor for my problems. I didn't mind; I got some positive attention out of it and a free ride out of class.

It was during this time in my life that I began to notice something unexplainable. Now and then, I would get up in the middle of the night to go to the bathroom or get a drink of water. As I walked through the dark house, I would get the feeling that someone was watching me, walking behind me. This presence was so strong that sometimes I would whip around, expecting someone to be there. But there never was. I wasn't afraid; I was just curious. After a while, I would just get up in the middle of the night to see if the presence would be there. It was. I continued to experience this presence off and on throughout the school year. The more it was around, the more I wanted it to be around.

Near the end of the school year, I noticed fliers being passed around school. They announced a Vacation Bible School being held at my elementary school. Games, food, and fun—this was for me! I took a flier home and gave it to my mother. To my complete surprise, she made a point of writing down the details of the VBS on our calendar.

School let out for summer, and shortly after, mom made sure I was on my way to VBS. I liked it right away. Just like the flier said, there were crafts, and cookies, and stories about a man named Jesus. I liked hearing about Jesus. They told me that He was the kind of friend someone like me could use. He was kind and caring and loved me. Then they asked us who would like to accept Jesus into his life. I shot my hand up right away. I wasn't sure what it meant to accept Him, but I knew that if anyone needed a friend, I did.

> **❝ Just like the flier said, there were crafts, and cookies, and stories about a man named Jesus. ❞**

Once Vacation Bible School was over, I wanted to continue my relationship with Jesus Christ, but I didn't know exactly what to do. At first I tried praying on my knees every day and reading the little King James Bible that I had been given, but I didn't understand the Bible, and after a while just put it on my night stand. I did continue talking to Jesus just as though He was walking with me and was my friend.

We had been in Marion just one year when my parents announced that we were going to move *again*. Getting out of town was becoming an annual event. So away we went—back to Upland. Well, at least I knew where we were going this time. Upland was okay with me.

We moved into a nice house this time. A much-respected family had previously occupied it. Maybe living there might change our reputation. Our new home was located right across the street from Taylor University, and the campus became my playground. This was great! I found that it was easier making friends, living on the "right" side of town. I was accepted and so was my family. Life began to seem better. I went to see my first movie. I joined a Little League baseball team. "Wow!" I thought, "Finally, life is going to be normal for us here!"

I didn't experience "the presence" at this house, but I did have an experience that shook me pretty well. It involved a Ouija Board. I don't remember exactly when we got it, but my family considered it "just a game." We would play with it and ask it questions, knowing that whatever sibling was playing, too, was moving the oracle back and forth among the letters and numbers to create outrageous answers. We enjoyed insulting each other through this game and would end up either fighting or laughing hysterically. I took the Ouija Board to my bedroom one night to play by myself.

"Let me see if this thing is real" I teased myself. I rested my fingers lightly on the oracle and asked my questions. The oracle began to move by itself. My body stiffened as I watched it answer one question after another.

Then a thought occurred to me. " Who are you?" I asked it.

The oracle spelled out " T H E D E V I L."

Scared to death, I threw the board across the room. I couldn't believe what had happened. When I calmed down, I realized that I was thrilled at the new reality of things unseen. It was just like when I had experienced the presence in our house in Marion. I became very interested in what had happened. My curiosity was piqued!

There had been just too many of these unusual types of things happening to me. I began to roll them over in my mind. First, the presence in our house in Marion. Well, that one was easy to chalk up to imagination. But THIS, this experience with the Ouija Board, was just too real to dismiss.

"I'm on to something," I thought. I wasn't sure exactly what, but I wanted to experience more of it.

The end of the school year was approaching fast and without being told, I knew what was going to happen. Yep, we were going to move. This was really getting old. I felt like a vagabond. I never had any friends for more than a year; I was in a new school every year. Why should I even try? No roots, no home, no friends. Why did my family have to be so different? I felt unstable. This time, we were moving to Hartford City. I didn't even wonder what was going to happen in this new town. I almost didn't care at this point. I felt numb from moving around.

When my parents finally announced our move, I began to disassociate myself with what I thought was the "good life" in Upland. I became sad, but just like every other year, I had to say good-bye. One night, about a week before we moved, I went to bed and something very interesting happened to me.

> **❝As I drifted off to sleep, I felt myself begin to leave my body.❞**

As I drifted off to sleep, I felt myself begin to leave my body. I drifted up toward the ceiling. Looking down, I saw myself lying on the bed. I felt lighter than air and could move about with ease. I started moving off in a certain direction as though being guided by someone I couldn't see. I floated through a house, examined each room, and committed it to memory. I went quickly through the living area and kitchen, glancing at the rest of the first floor. I made it back around to the stairwell and literally flew up the steps. I looked into the side rooms, and made a direct path into the room at the top of the steps. I had a settled feeling about that room. It was as if I belonged there. Suddenly and again, as if being guided, I found myself led back to my bedroom, where I lay asleep. I jerked awake, but quickly fell back to sleep.

Several days later, my parents gave us a chance to see the house into which we were moving. I had not been to Hartford City before, so I wanted the opportunity to see exactly what kind of town and house would soon be home.

"This is it?' I asked myself, looking out of the window in the car. I didn't like what I saw. Hartford City was a little larger than Upland. I knew that I wasn't going to like it here.

"Just once I would like to keep my friends! There is nowhere to play like there is at Taylor University." I thought angrily. "I don't want to stop playing little league with my team. They like me. I hate being in this family."

We pulled in the driveway and entered the new house. A shiver went up my spine. I had been there before. But when? I thought and thought, and then it hit me. This was the house in my "dream!" I looked around and realized that I knew exactly where everything was. Yes, there was the kitchen, the living room; the stairwell was right where I knew that it would be. "There's a room," I said to myself, "There's a room, and at the top of the stairs is ..."

"This is your bedroom," my mother announced.

I felt like my eyes were bugging out of my head, but I was too afraid to share my secret with my family. They would think I was crazy or lying. This was scary; this was thrilling! Once I was alone in my room, I thought, "I know that I'm on to something. But what? I don't know anyone to tell." I had to find an answer. But where?

# Chapter Four

**IN HARTFORD CITY, LIFE HAD** once again changed dramatically. I was only ten years old, and already my ability to roll with it was beginning to wear down. Even with the intrigue of having seen this new house in my dream, it wasn't nearly as nice as our previous house. Neither was the neighborhood. I felt as though I had taken a full step back. I could feel the anger beginning to burn inside me. How I wished that I belonged to another family! "Any family but this one," I thought. But, tired as I was of the emotional trauma, I was still just in elementary school and had no other place to go. I began to wish that I were dead. I felt as though I had been disappointed enough, and I was coming to terms with the fact that life wasn't going to get any better.

So, once again, that year I entered my new school with no friends, and had to start over at the bottom again. This time, however, I was quiet and withdrawn. I liked the school and the kids were okay, but why should I even try to attach to anybody? Instead, I dealt with living where I was by plugging into whatever activity I could. I joined the football league, but as much as I wanted to be good at this new sport, I really wasn't. Then I tried band, playing the drums. After that, I found basketball. I made the team at our school, but the first year was really humiliating—mostly because I was awful! What I really wanted was for my parents or someone to come and watch me play. But, no one ever came.

I decided that I would really try hard and practice at basketball. I became very attached to my coach. He was a sixth grade teacher and boy, did I want his attention. I was determined to improve. I practiced almost every day in order to improve. I was determined that the teacher was going to see me on the court as his most improved basketball player.

My teacher that year was the wife of a local pastor. Having her for a teacher reminded me about my relationship with Jesus and that maybe I should be in church. So I tried several different churches. These were the 1970s right in the heart of the "Jesus Movement," so knowing Jesus and anything Christian were very popular. There happened to be a Christian coffeehouse in our town called Jacob's Well, and Christian music was played openly on the radio stations.

Even with the "air" of Christianity everywhere, I wasn't having a positive experience in the church. I tried several different churches, hoping to fit in and to find a family. No one had time for a little boy who sat alone in a pew.

Life continued pretty much as usual that year. Soon November turned into December and just like any family, we started looking forward to Christmas. Somehow, even with the trauma of my life, this season always brought a renewed sense of hope. Up went the tree. Being a typical boy, I was drawn by the magnetic appeal of the presents underneath. Being drawn to the gifts led to an extraordinary experience, one that would help set me on a course of eventual destruction and ultimate salvation. I used to love to examine my wrapped presents for any hint of contents. I placed all my gifts in one spot so that on Christmas morning they would easily accessible. One present REALLY had my attention. It was the biggest. It was nicely wrapped, with a beautiful bow. I spent a lot of time just holding it. I hated the idea of not knowing the contents. One night I went to bed, and had another "dream" in which I saw the contents of the package. Inside were a pair of pants, a shirt, two pairs of socks, and a small black box in the corner. How amazing! I could see everything except what was in the black box. Then I woke up.

The next day I told my mother about the "dream" and what I had seen inside of the present. Instead of sharing my thrill of discovery, she got mad at me for opening my present before Christmas! I had been right! She wouldn't have been so enraged if I had been wrong. She grabbed the package and looked to see where I had opened it, but found that the paper and ribbon hadn't been disturbed. She must have been confused, but I was very clear. I had learned something important. I couldn't share my supernatural occurrences with my family. I knew that something big was happening. First, in an out-of-body experience, I had seen our house before we moved in. And now I had accurately seen the contents of my Christmas present before I opened it!

> 66 "Finally!" I thought, "Something positive is happening to me!" 99

"Finally!" I thought, "Something positive is happening to me!"

Life suddenly became exciting and filled with possibilities as if anything could happen! With no adult supervision from either my family or a community church, there was no one who knew that I had taken my first steps toward embracing the occult.

The end of the school year came and I felt myself bracing for our annual move. Much to my surprise, we stayed. The next year was my last year in elementary school, and it was actually a good one! I was doing okay socially and two years in a row in the same place felt like a lifetime.

As I entered my middle school years, I was again hit with a traumatic experience. For some reason in middle school, all of the kids from several elementary schools were combined and then divided according to achievement levels. I was excited because I had excellent grades in my 6th year and I knew that I would be put in good classes.

However, the children were not divided according to achievement, as we had been told happen. Instead, we were divided according to social class. Suddenly I found myself in a classroom full of kids that I didn't know. These kids were not doing well academically or socially. They were the outcasts and so, apparently was I.

This was a real blow to me. Being the child of an alcoholic is very demeaning. I had worked hard to make sure that I did my best. I had striven to attain the social status and acceptance that my shattered heart needed. This was the last blow. My heart was broken; I gave up. I stopped participating in sports. I stopped caring about grades. I quit band; I had never quit anything before. Now I was learning to quit and no one even noticed.

It was right about this time that I saw Uri Gellar on television, bending spoons with his mental powers. This reminded me of my own supernatural experiences. I thought that he was incredibly exciting. "If I could do this, too, that would be something!" I thought. So, I began to look for any available information at the library, but the library in our small town didn't offer much. I continued to see psychics and people such as Gellar and then famous Jeanne Dixon on television. I wanted what they had! In fact, I probably already had it! I was special and gifted. I knew that I had found just the thing to get me out of this social class where I knew I didn't belong. I knew that with this, I could get out of a town that I didn't want to move to in the first place, away from this family that I didn't feel connected to and on to a new and wonderful life.

# Chapter Five

**NOW, MY SEARCH WAS INTENTIONAL.** I was on to something. I looked for whatever it was that could cause my supernatural experiences to happen again. I wanted to know how I had left my body, how I could see my Christmas present, and who exactly the presence was that used to visit me at night. I used to watch "I Dream of Jeannie" and "Bewitched" on television, sure that we had something important in common, but unsure what.

I remained riveted on pop psychics, having identified them as the few people who were experiencing the same things I was. I was certain that I could find at least some answers by following them. I also found that as I pursued my new interest, Jesus didn't seem to be so important anymore. I was determined to find my answers in psychics and in the occult. "I'm done with the church," I thought to myself. "What has God done for me anyway?"

Depression and anger, which had previously drained me of energy, suddenly fueled my search for power and its mysterious source.

I began by reading a book on telepathy. It was very interesting and informative. It gave examples of personal experiences, and suggested experiments that would be easy enough to try at home. I recruited a friend. After school, we went to my house and sat facing each other. We got a deck of playing cards and each took turns looking at an individual card without showing or saying what it was. We then held the face of the card to our foreheads and concentrated on sending the information via thought to the other.

We took turns alternately. I looked at the card I held and then placed it on my forehead. I closed my eyes and concentrated very hard. Is the card red? Or black? I thought, "Black card, Black card, Black card." He got it wrong. Then I tried. I saw him look at the card and then place it on his head. I closed my eyes and went blank inside my mind. All of a sudden, I just knew it was a red one.

**❝Just like the people on TV! I can read minds!❞**

"Red," I said.

He opened his eyes amazed and turned over the card. It was red.

After numerous attempts, he had only gotten two right out of twenty attempts.

Out of that same twenty, I had identified eighteen. Amazingly accurate! What a feeling! "I have a gift!" I thought! "Just like the people on TV! I can read minds!"

I was very excited about the possibility of being able to read the thoughts of others; however, I found it difficult to find anyone who would take it seriously. All of my friends thought that it was a game, and either goofed around or got bored very quickly. My family ... well ... I just couldn't tell them anything. But this was no game. I discovered that when someone concentrated on sending me a message, I could receive it.

Disappointingly, I also found that I couldn't just go out into public and know what everyone was thinking. That would have been exciting. At least I was honing my personal skills, and I had a completely new sense of purpose, even if I didn't know exactly what to do with it.

It was during this time that my family and I moved yet again. This time, however, we at least stayed in the same town. We actually moved into a brand new house on a nice side of town! My dad bought a brand new car and we were able to get brand new clothes. Everything was new—except my attitude. By this point, I had left thoughts of a good family life far behind. I had seen this before and knew that it would be just a matter of time before things would fall apart again. I will admit that I did like the new house, car, and clothes. To a freshman in high school, these things are major factors in boosting self-esteem, but I knew that I couldn't trust the situation. So, I just took advantage of our new financial and social status while I could. I still just wanted out of my family.

Now that we had attained a better social status, I got to hang out with more of the "cool" kids and was invited to a lot of parties. I liked my new life! I learned things from my new friends. I learned to smoke cigarettes and drink beer, and I was pretty proud of it. It didn't take me long before I was smoking and drinking every weekend. After all, I had nothing else to do, and as angry as I was, no one could have stopped me.

After a while, however, I began to feel run down and tired. Then I began to get sick more frequently than usual. I found myself missing quite a bit of school. I was seeing the doctor often, but I wasn't getting any better. The doctor said that I had a blood condition and gave me frequent shots to help it. After months of shots and three different doctors, I showed no signs of improvement.

I can remember sitting in the last doctor's office in April, feeling like a balloon that was slowly deflating. As my mom and I walked to the car, I got angry. The three doctors were missing something. I saw that a new doctor had moved into the offices across the street. "That's where I want to go, Mom!" I said.

A short time later, I had an appointment with this new, young doctor from out of town. He actually listened to me and gave me an examination from head to toe. He immediately requested a thorough medical exam and chest x-rays, and met with me later to go over what he had found.

The results were not good. "You are in need of heart surgery," he said seriously. "The main artery in which blood flows out of your heart, your aorta, is closing down."

By May, I found myself in the Indianapolis Children's Hospital. The staff did an excellent job and it wasn't long before I had recovered enough to be sent home. I determined at this point that I was going to be "normal" as quickly as possible. I began to eat like a horse and quickly gained the weight back that I had lost. I rode my bike all over town that summer and in September, I even joined the cross-country team at school.

As I worked on my physical recovery, I also had to re-establish my social life. I stepped back into the party scene with new vigor after my surgery. I was determined to prove just how "cool" I really was. It wouldn't take me long to replace the "sick kid" image with the new and improved "party animal." So, I became the kid who was either drunk or high most of the time. Cigarettes and beer were passé to me now; I graduated on to hard liquor and marijuana. No one was as cool as I was. No one.

My parents seemed to be getting along better after my surgery. But it didn't take too long before they fell back into their old habits. By my junior year, they were worse that ever. I had grown so tired of the fighting and could only wait for them to divorce. Life wasn't going to be any better than what I could make it—and, I was determined to make it as good as I could by partying my way through high school.

# Chapter Six

**THE YEARS FOLLOWING MY SURGERY** were a mixture of anger and fear: anger for obvious reasons, fear because I should somehow have known what I was going to do after high school, but didn't. By my junior year, when all my friends and classmates were applying to colleges or making career plans, I still had no goals. I had never thought about it. I was too busy just trying to survive my home life and heart surgery. But now, ready or not, I had to make some kind of decision. I wasn't doing well academically, so college wasn't an option. I had no desire to be come a "blue collar" worker in one of the local factories. I felt trapped, and this only added fuel to my already smoldering anger. I felt very alone. There was no one with whom I could safely talk, so I started consoling myself in the only way that I knew. I followed in my father's footstep, only I didn't stop at drinking heavily; I added marijuana to the equation, and soon I was too numb to feel anything.

It was about this time that I discovered the band KISS. They really struck a chord with me because for the most part, their music felt as angry as I was. They seemed to capture my inner turmoil. They drew me like a magnet. I became interested in the 'character' that Gene Simmons played as a member of the band. He portrayed a demon. When I heard that they were performing nearby, I was there.

What an amazing night! I had never seen anything like it in all of the sixteen years of my life. They came out in an explosion of pyrotechnics. Their costumes made them a good six inches taller than the average person. Each musician played a different role on stage according to the makeup that he wore. As I expected, the demon/Simmons character was the strongest. It seemed to me that Simmons actually had "power" over his audience. He strutted on stage as the man "in control of it all."

Then they played the song, "God of Thunder." Simmons rose over the audience on a hydraulic lift. What I saw was the demon of the song coming to life, ruling over mankind. The impact of the vision he created with lyrics changed my life. He roared about being the lord of the wastelands who gathered darkness to please himself. His song ordered the listener to kneel before the god of thunder. He warned that the spell we were under would slowly rob us of our virgin souls.

**❝ He warned that the spell we were under would slowly rob us of our virgin souls. ❞**

As Simmons screamed these lyrics at the audience, most of us in our teens and early twenties screamed back at him in acceptance. This was the most power that I had ever seen before. Here, he was telling people that they were under a spell that would rob them, and they wanted even more! *I* wanted more! I wanted the power that Simmons seemed to have. If he had given an altar call for those interested in selling their souls to the devil that night, I would have run forward.

It was hard coming home to my life after catching a glimpse of all that I was seeking. I continued to experience premonitions (visions of things to come) and *déjà vu* (familiar feelings that one has already experienced a moment). These "abilities" at least kept pursuing an interest, but now I really wasn't satisfied. I could find no real answers in our small town library, even though I quickly read everything on the subject that they had. I wanted more than anything to encounter real live human beings who had similar experiences. I knew that I was gifted. I thought that I was a clairvoyant or at least that I had the potential for developing ESP, but had no direction.

In the middle of my junior year, my parents decided to divorce. Finally! It seemed that I had been waiting for this for years. I was so relieved! I thought back over all of the years of fighting and how I had given up the hope of ever having a happy family. I was so glad that this marriage was over and I could get on with my life.

Not long after the divorce, my mother went back to work. She came home every night talking about God and Jesus. I, however, wasn't listening. I had gone through enough, and was determined to seek my answers in the supernatural realm. I thought that I was going to find "deliverance" in being a psychic or clairvoyant. I wanted no part of God or the church.

One day my mother announced that she had become a "born again" Christian. I wasn't sure what this meant at first, but I quickly found out. Our household changed. Everything in our home suddenly revolved around Jesus! It seemed as though there were Bibles everywhere. There were pictures of Christian things on the walls. Christian television was on constantly, and so was Southern Gospel music. Then she began to pray with a friend in the kitchen every morning. I can remember feeling so uncomfortable that I began skipping breakfast or trying to sneak food out of the fridge to eat on the way to school. I used to stand just outside of the kitchen and reach around the corner in an effort to grab some kind of breakfast before she and her Christian friend would see me.

To my horror, my mom once said, "Jeff, I really think that God is going to use you to preach the Gospel one day."

That was **IT**! There was no way that I would ever let myself become so weak! Not long after that, I found myself watching one of those Christian television programs in disbelief. The preacher on the screen looked and acted like an idiot. The guy wore a polyester suit that was at least ten years out of date. On top of his head was a toupee so ill fitted and ill suited that it evoked both horror and embarrassment for him. It made me think that if he could pray for healing, he should pray for a cure for baldness or to be delivered from bad taste and no sense of style. He preached in an exaggerated southern accent that made him sound decidedly unintelligent. As if preaching badly were not enough, he escalated his pathetic performance by smacking people on the forehead and knocking them backward to the ground. This character then topped off his act with a plea for money from the audience in the studio and at home. I was not impressed.

> **❝I said, "God, if that's of You, I want NO part of You!"❞**

I said, "God, if that's of You, I want NO part of You!" But I meant that I wanted no part of Him at all. I had totally shut the door. He could knock on the door of my heart all He wanted, but it would not open ever again. Done, over, finished!

During my senior year I took a job as a stock boy in a local department store. Knowing that "real" life was going to start in the next nine months made me feel lost and confused. Well, at least I had a job!

I had a pretty good relationship with the people who worked in the store, but the assistant manager seemed to stand out from the beginning. He wasn't from my town, and there was a visible difference in his demeanor. He seemed to be a bit sharper than anyone I had met. He dressed well and commanded respect. He seemed to be in control of his life and on a path to personal success. I had been wishing for someone to step in with some answers to help guide me. So even though I felt inferior to him, I hoped that a working relationship would help me to become more like him. His name was Steve.

Winter that year was one of the coldest on record. In midwinter we were hit with a record-breaking blizzard. I was stuck at the store and frustrated because no one in my family would come out in it to pick me up after work. I was left to walk home through the arctic blast. Then to my delight, Steve offered to let me stay at his apartment for the evening. It was just around the corner. I took him up on his generous offer. Now I could stay warm and get to know my role model better. Possibly, even to learn something about the powerful authority he seemed to possess.

We walked to his apartment, stopping to pick up a six-pack of beer. As I entered his apartment, the hair on the back of my neck stood up. The same 'presence' that I had experienced all my childhood was there in his apartment. I knew that I wasn't there by chance.

Steve turned on the lights in the living room. I saw that his home was decorated with some unusual things. A ceramic skull graced the fireplace and a long wooden staff stood in the corner. We warmed up and settled in for the night.

Popping open a couple of beers we sat in front of the fireplace to talk. At first, the conversation was a little awkward but I couldn't contain my curiosity.

"What's the deal with the skull?" I asked.

He told me that he had noticed that I was interested the other things in his room as well. "Interested" was an understatement! He had the same 'presence' in his apartment that had followed me for years. Only here it was much stronger, and there was a sense of darkness more clear and distinct than I had ever known. I wanted to completely experience this darkness tonight.

**❝I wanted to completely experience this darkness tonight. ❞**

Steve politely told me about his skull candleholder, but I really didn't want to know about something so trivial. I knew that there was more here than met the eye, so I continued to probe Steve and found that he was very knowledgeable in the supernatural. He soon turned our discussion to the subject of the occult.

I found that we actually had a lot in common. He had the same desire to seek out the hidden things that I did. Soon he shared that he had found the way to 'tap into' the power or ability that I had been seeking. I was on the edge of my seat! Finally, here was someone with the answer! Here was someone who didn't dismiss my gifts as a lie or think that I was crazy. My body was tingling with anticipation.

"I'm a Satanist," Steve said in a matter-of-fact tone.

Somehow, I wasn't surprised. Steve told me that Satanism was the way to experience this supernatural reality on a daily basis. It seemed almost normal to me when he said that I could be taught how to exercise and expand my abilities. He told me that the answers to all of my questions would come from almighty Satan and that to be his disciple would be to have the power I had been longing for. I would know who I was, what I would do with my life, and how I would live. With this knowledge and power, I would be significant in my own eyes.

Then he invited me to become a Satanist. At that point, nothing could have held me back. I knew that this was my calling. We would sharpen our supernatural powers and become masters of our own destinies together.

Steve said that there was no need to wait. I could be initiated through ritual that very night. As we prepared for the ceremony, I shivered with cold excitement. I could feel every nerve tingling in anticipation of what was to come.

When we were ready, Steve started to pray over me and then laid his hands on me. As soon as he touched me, I experience the infilling of the demonic. I was experiencing demons inside of me for the first time. This was raw, uninhibited power. Their power became mine or so I thought. I didn't realize that I had just willingly stepped into a trap. And I had no idea what a sinister trap it was. I liked what I felt. I didn't feel alone anymore, because they were inside me and I knew it.

They actually moved my body at times. I could feel their thoughts and emotions. When I looked in the mirror, I could see them in my eyes. They gave me a sense that I was going to be a powerful human being. No more fearful little boy; now I lived with power! The god of thunder had me.

# Chapter Seven

**OVER THE NEXT SEVERAL DAYS,** I realized how different life was going to be from then on. The wait was over. With the help of my new spirit guides, I was going to grow in the abilities that had interested me all of my life. I had found my life calling. I didn't have to concern myself with college or factory work. I could relax and walk in the power that I had experienced the night of my initiation.

The first change that I noticed took place almost immediately. My view of life was different. My confidence had tripled. I felt in control and more aware of my surroundings than before. A spirit of pride had entered me and I knew that I would never fail. Now I determined what was mine. I came first. I was my own god. My friend Steve became my teacher, and I became his disciple. He became the one who took me by the hand, just as I had desired.

With my newfound "identity," I began to dress differently. Thanks to the influence of my friend Steve, I learned to pull my appearance together. Suddenly, I felt like showing off, and my peers thought that I was cool. The last part of my senior year was everything I had always dreamed—MY TIME. Finally, I would walk down the school halls and get the attention that I wanted. Students would comment on my cool clothes or laugh at my jokes. My social life kept improving, too. I no longer needed to go to the local parties; I was partying at the college in the next town over. This was a big deal in the eyes of an 18-year-old from a small town. It was also a big deal in the eyes of the "cool' kids at school. For the first time in my life, people looked up to me.

"This is my reward," I thought, "for being a Satanist.

I felt like life was so good at the time. I graduated that year very full of myself. I really believed that the world was mine. I couldn't fail, I was a god, and I had the power.

The day after I graduated, I moved out of my house. I didn't want to waste any more time. I didn't tell anyone where I was going. As far as I was concerned, I didn't need my family anymore. Steve and I took an apartment together in his hometown about forty-five minutes up the road. I felt released. I felt free to pursue Satanism with my whole heart, unencumbered by my mother's Christianity.

Steve and I delved into the books by the world's leading occultists. We focused on the writings of Anton LaVey, the founder of the Church of Satan. His self-serving approach to life intrigued me. I drank in the philosophy of Satanism, and loved the taste. I had felt and experienced the power. My mind was being renewed. I was thinking like a disciple. My special gift was the art of manipulation. I prided myself at being able to make people believe anything I wanted. This was power.

I was proud of my discipleship. I learned everything I could about my new approach to religion and life. I developed my own belief system and practices, and strove to adhere to them.

I was slowly, surely starting to think that my own beliefs were just as important as experiencing the demonic. The study of Satanism became my means of life.

I became a religious and philosophical Satanist. I remembered my experience on the night of my initiation, and hoped I would return to the supernatural realm soon. I really thought I was a higher-level person. I thought I was a much more intelligent thinker than the average person. I had a real superiority complex at the age of eighteen.

I was really enjoying life in this new town, too. I was free from the burden of my family. Here, no one knew who I was or had been. They didn't know that I was the son of the town drunk, and I didn't need to feel any shame. I thought that life was going to be better than ever. I thought life was going to be just as I had always wanted, and no one could take it away.

Little did I know that the God whom I had rejected would not be forgotten so easily as I wanted Him to be.

Steve's hometown was a quaint little Midwestern town. Cute little shops, not too far from a much larger college town, and ... full of Christians. As it turned out, the Christians in this town had such a strong presence that they seemingly knew exactly who was saved and who wasn't, and what was holding them back. To make matters worse, Steve's parents were a vital part of this group of Christians, and soon the Christian community in this town knew exactly who we were.

I was disgusted. I had just left the influence of my mother's newfound Christianity only to deal with the mature faith of Steve's parents. Why did I need to know that Jesus Christ loved me? I didn't believe it; I didn't want to hear it. From what I had read in the books on Satanism, these Christians were weak. Their spiritual view was backward. I just knew that my Satan had killed their Jesus, and that He was still dead, defeated. Why would I follow that loser?

But, not just Steve's parents told us about the love of Jesus. The church in which Steve had grown up and had at one time been a Christian was also assaulting us. They came after us like hounds on a fox's trail.

**❝It seemed that everywhere we went, a Christian would be there.❞**

It seemed that everywhere we went, a Christian would be there. At the grocery store. Pumping gas. I couldn't even take a walk in peace. Everywhere I went, someone would smile at me, or wave and say something like, "I'm praying for you!" Or "You know, Jesus loves you!" I met an old friend of Steve's, who ended up "sharing Jesus" with me. I was becoming more than upset at these Christians. To this point, I had just thought, "Live and let live." But now I looked at them as I would mosquitoes. They were buzzing, annoying pests that I needed to get rid of.

When I wasn't being "bugged," I really liked where I was living. In spite of the annoying Christians, I was starting to make friends and enjoy the place. Besides, *I* was the Satanist. *They* were the weak minded Christians. *I* was the one in control. After a while, though, Steve and I determined a counterattack to the Christian assault.

Over the next several days, we sharpened our plan. Steve said that we were going to "get back" at the Christians for relentlessly evangelizing to us. We were going to defile them. As forthright as they had been with their "holiness," we were going to invite them to be "unholy." "Let's see if they can walk the walk as well as they can talk the talk!" laughed Steve. The battle was on.

Steve came home one evening with a friend he had known back when they were both Christians. His friend, Brian, was still a practicing Christian and had no idea that Steve was a Satanist. Steve asked Brian if he would like some wine, and Brian, being polite, said, "Yes." I watched as Steve laughed and joked and politely caused Brian to get drunk and go against his own morals. We got him home and left poor Brian to deal with the repercussions of what had happened. This was going to be easier than I had thought it would be.

Up to this time in my life, I really had seen myself as a good guy. I had not really wanted to harm anyone, but these Christians were violating my self- absorbed life, and they needed to be put into their place. Besides that, who were they to be messing with me? I had experienced power from the demonic realm, and I was a foe to be reckoned with.

Next, Steve and I attended church just to preoccupy the minds of these Christians. We weren't really interested in what they were preaching and singing. They increased their effort in prayer because they were certain that we were going to go forth at some altar call, but no, we just wanted to play with them. We thought that it was fun messing with their minds. Besides, they couldn't touch us. Later, however, I would discover exactly how effective the prayers of the saints are.

# Chapter Eight

**AS THE BATTLE CONTINUED,** we became obvious in our rejection of Christianity. The Christians continued their attempts to befriend us, but the more they pushed me to "know Jesus," the more I desired to delve into Satanism. They angered me. I had a great desire to put these Christians and their "religion" to rest. I wanted to destroy them. What right did they have to interfere in my self-absorbed life anyway? No one was going to take anything away from me anymore. These Christians were violating my right to choose who I wanted to serve and how I wanted to live.

The Christians in this town angered us so much that we decided to move to another town. We were going for a new identity and a deeper walk in Satanism. We began to seek the power of the demonic realm. We also began to talk about getting others involved. There was a new focus on what we were doing.

With our new resolve and enthusiasm to grow as Satanists, we began to do a bit of evangelizing. We started by throwing parties and supplying everyone with the means of having one "hell" of a good time. We presented ourselves as people who "had it all." Then we concentrated on raising a coven of men who would serve Satan. One by one, we gained new members who served us as they served Satan. We were no longer interested in philosophical or religious angles. We were after power. We gave all to serve the god of this world, and we believed that he would reward us for being faithful servants.

Evangelizing was surprisingly easy. We had recruited a group of seven in a few weeks. Our new members were young men from respected families. They included the son of a lawyer and the son of the basketball coach, for example. No one could have guessed that they were Satanists. These new coven members were as eager to join as I had been. They came in with high hopes for purpose and self-fulfillment in life. They believed that they were going to become powerful Satanists and be in control of their futures. Together, we would fulfill our black destinies.

> **❝ One by one, they became demon-possessed just as I had. ❞**

I watched them as they began to idolize Steve and me. I believed that it was part of my destiny to have people look up to me. It only reaffirmed my self-absorption. I didn't mind at all that in their eyes, I had become more than I really was. I enjoyed it. I thrived on it. Somewhere deep inside, though, I knew that I had nothing worthy of anyone's worship.

I also watched as, one by one, these young men went through their initiation into Satanism. One by one, they became demon-possessed just as I had. And just as I had, they readily offered themselves to Satan, believing that their souls and bodies would be amply rewarded. I watched as they changed from young men to demon-possessed souls. Somewhere along the line, I started to regret what I was doing to them. I was starting to feel a bit concerned for them, and it surprised me. I scoffed,

"Why should I care about these young men and their lives?" After all, I was out for number one—myself.

It wasn't too long after this that we were able to move into a larger house. With the added financial support of the new coven members, it was easy. This beautiful old home had enough rooms in it for most of us to live together and create a ritual chamber. We were able to focus on ceremonies and rituals, and develop our brand of Satanism.

By day, we worked regular jobs and paid our bills. We were upstanding members of the community. By night, we performed rituals. We gave ourselves over to Satan's power with a militant passion. We were deadly serious in our intention and each one of us was rewarded with a serious experience of the demonic in one manner or another. As we gained in experience, we learned how to exercise the abilities that our demons gave us.

My personal experience was to have the demons living in me. This meant that I would allow any part of my soul that might be considered good to die. I sacrificed my heart and any love that was in me in exchange for more of Satan's abilities. I thought that there was nothing more thrilling than to experience demonic control. I welcomed them. I was able to know their thoughts and feel their emotions. At times, their personalities would become my own. This oneness with the demons was the ultimate prize. The more that I gave myself to them, the more they would control me.

However, when it came to the younger members of the coven, I started to experience a real struggle within my soul again. Had I not been a Satanist, I might even have called it "remorse." Steve had set himself up as the unapproachable leader of our group. This way, he inspired awe and respect; younger members would more easily follow him. His only interaction with the younger members was when they were being taught or it was time for a ritual. Even during social times, Steve was to be adored and worshiped. He wasn't their friend, and I soon lost him as my friend, as well. Because of this estrangement, I became the man in charge of the new inductees. If they had an issue, they came to me. They were young and had normal struggles with life, not to mention struggles with their new satanic lifestyle. I, in essence, became a father figure and friend to them. In return, I felt myself beginning to care for and about them. I was very frustrated at this attribute within me. Caring for others is a character flaw if you are following Satan. Apparently, my heart wasn't completely dying as I had hoped.

About this time, Steve let me know that as a group, we were almost at a place where we could divide and multiply. He said that as I had been personally discipled for a few years, I should be preparing myself mentally and spiritually to start my own coven. I was to be a priest in training and should be ready to start my own coven within the next year.

This was a boost to my ego. I really liked the sound of having my own coven. So, I began to intensify my efforts to deaden my heart, especially in the area of caring about anyone or anything but myself. I had a renewed since of urgency. I was going to die to love and let the unholy spirit rule within me.

# Chapter Nine

**IF I HAD BEEN INTENSELY DEVOTED** to Satan before, I was even more so now. I was determined. I would show myself to be as powerful and in control as I possibly could. I would do this for me. No one would stand in my way. I believed that I had a great future with my master Satan. I wanted to be adored and looked up to just as Steve was within our coven. I decided to expand my future professionally, as well. I enrolled in college with what I thought was a clear picture of my glorious future in mind.

By this time, all of the younger members of our coven had graduated from high school. One by one, we enrolled in college. Our plan was to become well educated and respected in our chosen professions. All of us except one. There was one young man who wasn't going to get an education. I'm sorry to say that we had a "worker" in our coven, who was being used. He would work all week and give his paycheck to Steve and me. He got us whatever we would tell him to, from beer to marijuana. Steve and I didn't look upon him as an equal. He was there in the role of a servant, and he served us well. We were Satanists. We were not nice, and we used him.

I began my studies and was immediately drawn to the social sciences. I was intrigued with history, as well. I saw that history was more than dates and places. These were the tales of individual lives that were collectively recorded. Real people fought the wars, and I found their personal lives very interesting. I became fascinated with sociology and began to look through the eyes of sociology to see individual lives of humanity.

My next interest was psychology. It really grabbed hold of me, and I chose it for my major. I narrowed in on the study of the individual. I needed to know more about things that matter to the human spirit and heart. The area that seemed to fascinate me the most was child development. I was

> **❝I thought life was finally coming together ... at least on the outside.❞**

convinced that this is what I wanted to do with my life. I would be a child psychologist and a Satanist! I felt like a walking oxymoron. How amazing that even though I didn't know it, I was feeling the gentle tug of the life God had intended for me—helping people.

At the start of the school year, I came into some unexpected money. I just knew that my service to Satan was paying off. The first thing that I did was to purchase a beautiful diamond ring that I personally designed. What a boost to my overly inflated ego! Then I began to upgrade my wardrobe and to dine in the restaurants about which I had only dreamed a child. I really thought I was something! I thought life was finally coming together ... at least on the outside. I also thought what I was feeling on the inside would soon be dead, so I continued to ignore my growing conscience.

I wanted power and position. I had attained a level of power through Satanism. I was content with my position in life as a college student aspiring to be a professional and having my own coven. I was able to resist entertaining these desires and thoughts at least while I was around my coven and Steve. It was much easier to focus on evil when I was with my peers. But, my heart began to yearn for something outside of my evil companions, even though I kept pushing it down inside me. I was surprised to find that I wanted to fall in love and have a family. I had suppressed these thoughts for a long time. I tried my best to resist. However, when I was alone, I would catch myself imagining what life would be like with a wife, family, and love. I started to realize that although I had stepped into some money, it didn't purchase my happiness. I continued to wrestle with my heart, which seemed refused to die. With all that I had given to Satan, my heart should have been dead by now. Frustratingly, maybe I was human after all.

At this point, I was thoroughly confused. I now had everything for which I had hoped. The better life, about which I had dreamed as a child, didn't seem to really be better. I was still wrestling with my search for fulfillment. To make matters worse, I found that the demonic abilities that were my strength and pride were starting to diminish. I was losing my powers. This was completely unacceptable to me! So, I let go of my romantic notions and approached Satan with a ritualistic fervor. I did everything that I could think of to sharpen my relationship with the unholy, including desecrating the most powerful church in the area. "That should do it!" I said to myself, but nothing changed. I was infuriated! I had given my life to Satan; why should he pull back from me? I needed some answers.

Steve and I had been growing apart for some time. I no longer looked upon him as my teacher or even as my friend. But, like it or not, I needed some answers, so I told Steve what was happening to me. I let him know how angry I was, and that I desired to experience my abilities again so that I could take the larger step forward toward gaining my own coven. I didn't want to waste any more time.

The answer that Steve gave me just about flipped me out. He said that my powers were dimensioning because angels were stopping them. He said that I was "angelically oppressed!"

"How could this be?" I thought, "Christians don't have this kind of power! Besides, Jesus is dead!" It just seemed too farfetched. I couldn't grow if I wanted to. This was unbelievable! Now, I wasn't only wrestling with my undying heart and romantic notions, I was also wrestling with angels! What in the world happened to the better life that I was trying to attain?

We immediately held a ritual in order to cause the situation to change, but the ritual didn't yield results. I wanted something to happen immediately. I began to search inside of me for possible reasons that I could be hindered. I looked for the reasons that the rituals, which I performed with such fervor, were ineffective. Maybe it was because I desired a close relationship with another human being or even a woman. Maybe my dreams of being a husband and father were the keys. Why wasn't my heart dying to these aspects? Why wasn't I more of a personification of the demons that lived inside me? The thing that really stumped me, though, was how angels could have access to me. How were they allowed to hang around me, much less "bind" any one of my powers? As far as I knew, Jesus was dead. He had died on the cross and that was the end of him. I was the one serving the god of this world. I thought that Christianity was a joke and that I could live my life as I had planned it. But apparently not. I was being stopped in my tracks. I was going absolutely nowhere.

My schoolwork began to suffer because of my confusion. I grew disinterested in my classes and couldn't focus on studying or anything else. I took long walks and thought a lot about my life. I found no satisfaction in the things that my money had been purchasing. I knew I needed a change, but I wasn't sure exactly what change I needed.

Because the demons inside me were no longer able to "act out" and torment others through me, as they desired, they tormented me instead. I was miserable! I had a hard time sleeping, and there was nowhere that I could go to be alone with my thoughts. Suddenly, Satanism wasn't serving me any longer. On the contrary,

**❝When I got into Satanism, I had no idea that Almighty God could stop me.❞**

he was turning against me. The longer I went, the more confused I became. I wanted to scream and throw something; often I did. When I got into Satanism, I had no idea that Almighty God could stop me. I had no idea that the Christians whom Steve and I had often ridiculed could hinder us with their prayers. I had no idea what a slim chance we had at ever being successful Satanists.

I was too engrossed in my lifestyle to figure out that if Jesus was the one who was stopping me, maybe He was the one that I should be serving. Instead, I became increasingly angry. I chose to die. I had given my life to Satan and tasted what I believed was the real power that could get me where I thought I wanted to be in life. But, even in my experience as a Satanist, I found that my heart lived on. I found that I wanted to fall in love and have a family. On top of the angelic oppression, I felt like life had become simply frustrating. I would show Jesus and everyone else who my lord was. So, death would be the best answer.

We had talked often in our coven about offering a sacrifice to Satan. We began discussing this a lot more earnestly now. I decided to step forward and volunteer to be the blood sacrifice. I honestly believed that if I offered myself to Satan as a sacrifice that I would be rewarded in the afterlife by reigning in Hell. I would get myself out of this awful dilemma, and be the ultimate servant of Satan. I knew that this was my best option. I began to prepare myself spiritually for my ascension.

To my dismay, Steve refused my offer. He wouldn't even consider me as a sacrifice! This was a real slap in the face. I wondered why I wasn't counted worthy of such an honor. This rejection only made matters worse for me. My life became living hell. I was being tortured on the inside and oppressed on the outside. Now, I had been refused the opportunity to die an honorable death. I could see that I was on my own. I would not get answers from anyone around me. I needed a way out, and I wasn't sure which way to go, or what exactly to do. But given time, I knew I would figure it out.

# Chapter Ten

**DEATH WAS THE ONLY SOLUTION.** Not only was I battle weary, but also I was just plain tired of life. Nothing had worked, and I was heartbroken. As unbelievable as it sounded, Satanism had not given me what I desired. I had experienced the power of demons and darkness. I had achieved a level of prosperity and position within my coven. But, the cold reality was that I couldn't purchase or induce through ritual or manipulation what I really wanted. I wanted to love and be loved. With that realization, I was angered at the weakness of my heart.

So, I gathered my strength, went to the local pawnshop, and purchased the gun that hopefully would put my soul to rest. I told the pawnshop owners that there had been an attempted burglary at my house the previous night and that I needed this gun for protection. In my mind, I had a vision of the newspaper article that would announce my suicide. I pictured the surprise of this simpleminded store owner when he saw my face next to the story. I thanked them for the gun and walked down the street to the nearest hotel. I put the gun in the bushes and went in to get my room. The clerk, courteous and efficient, could never have guessed that I planned to use this room to end my life. With my key in hand, I went to the bush to collect my gun, entered the room, and began to unpack a brown paper bag that I had brought with me. It contained whiskey and marijuana to give me the strength to do what I needed to do.

I sat on the bed drinking and smoking myself into a place of inner courage. I convinced myself that this needed to happen. As I **❝… for some reason, I was** put the barrel against my **afraid of my eternal destiny** head, I felt a wave of fear. **and I didn't know why.❞** The weird part of it was that I really wasn't afraid to die. I got the overwhelming concern for where I would go after I was dead! "Why am I concerned about this?" I asked myself. I thought that I *wanted* to reign in Hell with my master Satan. But now, for some reason, I was afraid of my eternal destiny and I didn't know why. This fear was powerful enough to stop me from taking my life that night.

The next morning I woke up and went to the home that Steve and I shared with two other members of the coven. Everyone had gone either to work or to his college classes, so I found myself alone. In this solitude, I began to contemplate my situation. Now that I was completely sober and in my right mind, it seemed so ridiculous that I had attempted suicide, only to be stopped by my fear of the afterlife. I resolved right then to make another attempt to take my life. I would hang myself.

I went to my garage where I found some rope and tied a noose. Since no one was around to stop me, I was sure that my little scheme would take care of everything. I threw the rope over the garage rafter and tied it as tightly as I could. I placed the noose around my neck. I was prepared to die. Wrestling with the issue of my eternal destiny was meaningless. I kicked the chair out from under my feet, anticipating that the jerk on my neck that would bring my life to a sudden end.

For an instant, I felt the rope tighten. Then just as quickly, I fell to the floor of the garage.

After regaining my breath, I sat up on the floor and looked up at the rafter that I had thought would bring me relief

**"How could I fail at suicide—not just once, but twice?"**

from life. I couldn't believe that I was still alive. How could I fail at suicide—not just once, but twice? It seemed that the old saying, "When it rains, it pours," was becoming my reality. It was pouring misery for me.

Eventually the other members of the coven came home from school and work. Steve immediately saw that I was in turmoil. So, he gave the order for us to have a party! He didn't want the younger members of this group to find that Satanism wasn't working for his priest in training.

Steve sent our coven worker to get plenty of alcohol for our party. There was tension in the air, so Steve lit up some marijuana and began to get the younger members of the coven high. I didn't smoke any. I had no desire to party. I just wanted to die.

When the alcohol did arrive, I found that the smell of the beer literally nauseated me. I picked up someone else's beer and it smelled as bad as mine did. Cigarettes and marijuana also sickened me.

I was amazed and perplexed that I couldn't turn the night into a drunken, drug-crazed stupor. I was totally aware of the fact that my every attempt was being overridden. I was losing control. I couldn't succeed at being a Satanist, offering myself as a sacrifice, suicide, or even intoxicating myself. I was a total failure.

After a while, the rest of the group decided to go to a party at the college campus. I stayed back, explaining that I didn't want to party, and that I just wanted to be left alone. I walked around the house by myself for a little while, too emotionally spent to think. I was exhausted. I decided to go to bed to get some sleep. As soon as my head touched the pillow, an overwhelming grief took over and I began to cry uncontrollably. It was then that I heard the voice of the Lord speak the words "Get Out!" I crawled out of my bedroom window and met Jesus Christ in my backyard!

There I was, on my face in front of the garage where I had tried to kill myself. I'm not sure how long I remained in the presence of the Lord. But I do know that when I finally got up and went back inside of the house, I had changed. I immediately went to bed and slept peacefully all night.

The next morning, I opened my eyes and remembered my encounter. I wasn't the same. As the next few days passed, I felt a real separation from my satanic comrades. I had absolutely no desire to drink, smoke, or do any kind of partying with them. I began to quietly separate myself from them, not fearfully, but wondering what I should do next. I didn't tell them. I knew what their reaction would be, and it didn't scare me. I just didn't feel like I needed to say anything just yet.

About a week later, I went down into the basement to do some laundry. As I was working, I heard footsteps coming down the stairs. It was Steve, and he wasn't happy. With fire in his eyes, he began to ask some pointed questions about my lack of participation in the group's activities. I calmly answered his questions one after another. He continued to badger me, and the more he talked, the angrier he became. Finally, after several minutes of heated discussion and accusation, he asked, "What god do you serve?"

I stood up straight and turned to face him. Looking him right in the eye, I firmly answered, "Not yours."

Steve punched me so hard that I flew across the room and landed on the floor. He glared at me angrily and stormed up the stairs. As I slowly stood, I rubbed my aching jaw to see if it was broken. Thankfully, it wasn't. Then the thought occurred to me, "Is that all he's got?" He had just lost his power over me.

Just a few days after this incident, the coven moved out of the house and left me there to finish out the lease alone. They just left me! So, I was free to reacquaint myself with this God whom I was serving without any interference. But where to begin? I thought, "Well, I know that Christians go to church, so maybe I should go to church."

And so the search began. I visited church after church, most of which seemed to be more interested in their programs and buildings than in the reason for my visit. I eliminated them all until I was down to the last church, one that I would never have chosen on my own. It was a very small church full of loving people and the Spirit of the Lord. Somewhat embarrassed, I looked around the place and smiled to myself. This was the very church that I had desecrated in my anger. I got some peculiar looks as I walked in, because of the tinted glasses I wore. My eyes had become light sensitive, and I had an unhealthy appearance. I tried to hide in the back pew; it's hard to be inconspicuous in such a small church. Then I began to feel increasingly uncomfortable because the demons inside of me were uncomfortable. There was great struggle going on within me. They wanted me to leave and harassed me relentlessly. They made me as miserable as possible while I was in church.

After I had made it through the sermon, a loving Christian couple walked up to me and invited me to their house for dinner. I could hardly look them in the eyes, but my heart jumped at the opportunity to have human contact, so I accepted. Their names were Harry and Jo Richardson.

A few days later I found myself seated rather awkwardly in the beautifully furnished home of two retired Ball State faculty members. Harry had been a head librarian and Jo had been an art professor. We ate a wonderful homemade meal of ham loaf and baked yams. As I sat at the dinner table, the demons inside of me were squirming. Personally, the profound peace and quiet of their home made me want to scream! However, I wanted human contact more than I wanted to run, so I stayed.

After dinner, Jo moved us into the living room and began to ask me who I was and where I had come from. We didn't get too far into our conversation when I couldn't keep my secrets one minute more.

"I think you need to know that for the past four years, I've been a Satanist!" I blurted out. I couldn't believe that I had said it.

It didn't take Jo more than two seconds to decide what to do. Standing up, she grabbed my hand and pulled me off the couch to stand next to her. As Harry came to his feet, she looked me in the eyes and said, "Oh, then you need prayer!"

Jo and Harry Richardson began to pray. I don't remember what exactly they said except that I distinctly remember Jo mentioning the Blood of Jesus. I do know that as they began to pray, the demons that were living in me turned my head to look at her. When they did, for a moment I saw what they saw and felt what they felt. I saw the most powerful steel blue eyes that I had ever seen. They were at the same time powerful and loving. For just an instant, as I looked into her eyes, I felt overwhelming fear. And then suddenly the demons left me. I took a deep breath. I could hardly believe it. I was free!

**❝I started laughing and ran to the bathroom to look at my eyes. There I was! It was me!❞**

I started laughing and ran to the bathroom to look at my eyes. There I was! It was me! I had become so accustomed to seeing demons in my eyes, and they were not there! For the first time in years, I looked into the mirror and saw me! I must have smiled for a month solid afterward.

Back in the living room, Jo and Harry were laughing and praising the Lord. What a wonderful thing they did when they obeyed God and invited me to dinner.

That invitation started a relationship, which the Lord used to help set me free. Harry and Jo became like parents to me. Through them, I received unconditional love and endless counsel. I knew that I had spiritual family to whom I could turn in my greatest need.

Over the next few years, the road that I walked wasn't an easy one, but thanks to my new family, I had a safe place to go when I needed it. As Harry and Jo mentored me, I began to grow stronger as an individual and as a

Christian. They worked hard to teach me the Word of God and how to live it. It's their example that I strive to imitate to this day.

God has revealed Himself to me—not in some sensational way—but in the only way that I would receive Him. I was stubborn enough to have come to a place of attempting suicide before I would accept His gift of eternal life.

He has shown Himself to be faithful. "God is faithful, by whom you were called into the fellowship of His Son, Jesus Christ, our Lord" (1 Corinthians 1:9). His character is defined by the reality of this passage. He can be trusted, because He is who He says He is and does what He promises He will do.

Hebrews 13:5b states, "For He Himself has said, 'I will never leave you, or forsake you.'" He doesn't walk away from me. I haven't found Him to be a liar, either. I can take Him at His word and so can you. He has done exactly what He has said that He would.

The night that I asked Jesus Christ for help, He helped me. It hasn't been easy, but He has been my refuge and strength, a very present help in trouble. (Psalm 46:1,2)

All that He has done for me, He WILL do for you. I'm telling my story to encourage and strengthen anyone who will listen. Satan is defeated; Jesus is not dead, but lives. He has changed my life. He can change yours, too. I know. I'm living proof. Today, I devote my life to rescuing other people. My wife Liz and I head Refuge Ministries, a program that offers biblical counseling and help to those in need. Our phone never stops ringing, and we never tire of lecturing and counseling with people all over the world who summon us for help or travel to us when they need to be delivered from darkness.

Over the years, I've learned through experience that my story is not unique. Many people have embraced the loving grace of Jesus Christ after living in the occult. I have also learned that there are just as many who are still in the occult and are looking for truth or a way out. These people may be alone in their quests or be held faithfully in prayer by a concerned friend or family member. In any instance, the only way out of the occult is through a relationship with Jesus Christ.

I've told you my story because it has a happy ending that can be yours, too. If you have a loved one mired in the dark forces of the occult, you can help lead him or her out. The next section of this book will teach you to recognize the traps set by Satan, and then show you how to rescue someone you love with the Lord's help. Let's get started.

# Part Two

# Quick study of the occult

# Chapter Eleven

# General Introduction

**IN THIS SECTION OF THE BOOK,** we'll look at various beliefs and practices within the occult. We'll also examine the common myths, misunderstandings and mistakes. I'll teach you how to approach and help those who are in this trap. I would urge you to use a highlighter and take notes or earmark the section(s) that pertain to you.

We need to understand that every area of the occult has subgroups, and as many different beliefs and practices as there are groups or individuals—literally thousands. And so, addressing EVERY practice and belief would be an exhaustive study and would fill a much larger book than this. I want to give you a general, but firm foundation in understanding occultic beliefs and practices, and show how to approach its members with love and the redeeming features of our Lord Jesus Christ. (We'll do this is Section Three.)

Before you turn the page however, we need to address two common misapplications of the authority of the believer in the areas of our study.

A good number of believers that we've met, upon coming face-to-face with the topic of the occult, react in one of two ways: fear or pride.

## FEAR

People who fear cause doubt in the Body of Christ. They are afraid that somewhere, somehow, by willful association (having contact with occult members) or even just touching a particular item, a demon will attach itself in an attempt to wreak havoc in his or her home and thwart all evangelistic efforts toward the person they are trying to rescue. These fearful Christians pray the same prayers of deliverance repeatedly and constantly, anoint themselves with oil, even sleep with the light on. While it's true that a demon might follow you home if you are in sin (spiritual pride is a good example), Scripture is very clear and in your favor:

> *"Therefore submit to God, resist the devil and he will flee from you" (James 4:7 NKJV).*

There are no "ifs, ands or buts" to God's Word, and the devil knows it. There is no need to fear. If you are afraid, then God is not in control of your life. We need to spend more time meditating on God's Word, ridding our hearts of sin by repenting daily to our Lord, and loosing the fear by focusing on His provision. If you ask Him, He will tell you where you are missing it. We all need to be listening to the testimonies of believers and simply spending time with God: talk, listen, and read His Word. If you have a hard time remembering what He says, I would recommend keeping a journal. As long as you are right with the Lord, in all humility and taking direction from Him, you will be fine.

You must also understand that God has already won this war for us when He died on the cross and rose from the grave. WE do nothing; GOD does everything. Satan is already defeated.

*"For in Him dwells all the fullness of the Godhead bodily; and you are complete in Him, who is the head of all principality and power. In Him, you were also circumcised with the circumcision made without hands, by putting of the body of the sins of the flesh, by the circumcision of Christ, buried with Him in baptism, in which you also were raised with Him through faith in the working of God, who raised him from the dead. And you being dead in your trespasses and the uncircumcision of your flesh, He has made alive together with Him, having forgiven you all trespassed, having wiped out the handwriting of requirements that was against us, which was contrary to us. And He has taken it out of the way, having nailed it to the cross. Having disarmed principalities and powers, He made a public spectacle of them triumphing over them in it"* (Colossians 2:9-15).

Satan likes to trick people into thinking that he is in more control than he really is. When his deception succeeds, we begin to discount God's victory. This creates doubt in the Almighty God. We stop believing Scripture in our hearts. It is then that we submit to fear.

## PRIDE

Proud Christians are flawed Christians. They might very well understand the defeat of the devil by Jesus' cross and resurrection, but pride keeps them from being able to rescue effectively. In fact, they inflict a lot of damage on the new or prospective convert. Rigid in their thinking and arrogant in their theology, they tend to make up their own ways to deliver people. Most of these ways are completely non-biblical and without the guidance of the Holy Spirit. If their well intentioned, but inept methods weren't so damaging to the individual, they would be laughable. I have seen people hit on the head with the Bible (unbelievable!), and told to vomit the devil out (no kidding!).

I know a teenager on medication who was told that the reason that she was always sleepy was that a Demon of Tired possessed her! No mention was made of the effects of the medication. This poor kid was afraid to go to sleep for months afterward.

I even once witnessed a Christian look into the eyes of a poor soul and in a very loud voice, command a Spirit of Diarrhea, "Come out in Jesus' name!" The person was mortified, and all the ushers reacted by stepping back three feet. (It was a good thing for us that this deliverance minister was wrong, or we would have had a clean up on Aisle Seven!)

Proud Christians help to create the Christians who react in fear. As I've said, they're almost always well intentioned, but in their pride, they are usually just a little loud and just a tad bit showy. I'm reminded of what Jesus had to say about public displays of religion:

> *"Take heed that you don't do your charitable deeds before men, to be seen by them. Otherwise, you have no reward from your Father in heaven. Therefore, when you do a charitable deed, don't sound a trumpet before you as the hypocrites do in the synagogues and in the streets, that they may have glory from men. Assuredly, I say to you, they have their reward.*
>
> *But when you do a charitable deed, don't let your left hand know what your right hand is doing. That*

*your charitable deed may be in secret: and your Father who sees in secret will Himself reward you openly.*

*And when you pray, you shall not be like the hypocrites. For they love to pray standing in the synagogues and on the corners of the streets that they may bee seen by men. Assuredly, I say to you, they have their reward.*

*But you, when you pray, go into your room and when you have shut your door, pray to your Father who is in the secret place and your Father who sees in secret will reward you openly"* (Matthew 6:1-4 NKJV).

I cannot stress enough how critical it is to walk humbly before the Lord. Many new believers have simply slid into quiet suffering because they have been "slam-dunked" by someone who has done something awful to them or has required that they fit a certain mold before they are ready. Yes, coming out of the occult *does* require a lot of change. **But you and I can't do it.** It's best to keep our mouths shut, teach by example, pray humbly, and watch the Master do what He does best: create a new heart.

Now, with that having been said, let us proceed.

# Chapter Twelve

# General Overview of the Occult

**WEBSTER'S DICTIONARY DEFINES** the word "occult" in this manner: **Oc.cult 1**. Adj. beyond the range of normal perception// secret, mysterious, esoteric //dealing with magick, divination, and spiritism // 2. n. (with "the") supernatural.

And so our study begins.

All of the belief systems defined here fall under the general heading of "occult." Although beliefs and practices may vary from group to group, a link connects them all:

**the quest for hidden knowledge, or the claim to possess hidden knowledge.**

The draw of the occult began in the garden where Adam and Eve questioned God's Word. In the third chapter of Genesis, the serpent questions God's Word by asking:

*"Has God indeed said, You shall not eat of every tree of the garden?*

*And the woman said to the serpent, We may eat the fruit of the trees of the garden; but of the fruit of*

*the tree which is in the midst of the garden, God has
said, You shall not eat it, nor shall you touch it, lest
you die.*

*And the serpent said to the woman, You will not
surely die, for God knows that in the day you eat of
it your eyes will be opened and you will be like God,
knowing good and evil" (Genesis 3:2-5).*

Satan cast doubt on the Word of God in an attempt
to negate God's character so that man would reject God
as One worthy of worship and trust. Without the
Almighty, man then had to place himself as the object
of worship and trust. Man became his own god, and the
result was self-centeredness. Then Satan misrepresented
God's provision and protection so that man would see
them as imperfect, and feel as though he must provide
for and protect himself.

By misrepresenting God and tempting human beings
to rebel against Him, Satan undermines our relationship
with Him. Instead of man being a reflection of the perfect
Almighty God, and in this, having all desire fulfilled,
the occult steps in as man's provision for fulfillment. In
place of an intimate relationship with God, man's quest
to be perfect, as God is perfect, becomes instead a quest
to be a god: to have hidden **knowledge**, which is the
very definition of the occult.

This romance with all things "hidden" makes many
occultists feel as though they are a special, separate, and
uniquely intelligent group of individuals. They like to
believe that they are set apart from the "common man."
Certainly, they are above religions they consider to be
obsolete, ineffective or adulterated. This includes, but
doesn't necessarily single out, Christianity. In reality,
many occultists will take on a "hidden" life—not real,

but created to complete the imagined god-hood. They will often project the illusion of a persona, a masquerade of who they *want* to be, so that they can hide who they really are.

As a Christian, the most important step in approaching an occultist is to reflect God's character. Keep in mind that misrepresentation of God's character is one of the reasons individuals to pursue the occult; they don't know God and what He can do. Moreover, they feel deceived by the misinformation and perception of hypocrisy that makes God seem very distant, if real at all. When someone is in search of spiritual meaning, and God is apparently not the answer, then the search turns elsewhere. And where more obvious than the occult?

It gets worse. Misrepresentation is also one of the greatest impediments to rescue. It assaults our credibility and sets up a lack of trust that's nearly impossible to overcome. We'll go into this in detail later.

# Occult Practices

All of the occult practices fall into one or a combination of these three categories:

### Magick (sorcery)
**Manipulation and control of people, nature, and circumstances through the knowledge and control of the spirit world.** An example of this would be the rituals that I performed as a Satanist in order to change a circumstance or to bring into existence good fortune. In contrast, God revealed Himself in Scripture teaching us to submit to Him and to trust Him.

## Divination (fortune-telling)

**Seeking hidden knowledge not easily available to humans.** For example: astrology (horoscopes) and reading your horoscope in an attempt to find out what your future holds. Also includes reading tea leaves and palms of hands.

## Spiritism (necromancy)

**Contact with the unknown in order to gain desired knowledge.** For example: John Edwards and Sylvia Brown, mediums between the living and the dead. Other seemingly innocent practices that fall under this category are the Ouija board and séances.

In the next few chapters, we'll be addressing the beliefs and practices of various forms of occultism. We will be clarifying some misinformation and common myths propagated by uninformed sources.

This is the real thing.

# Chapter Thirteen

# Satanism

**GENERALLY SPEAKING, SATANISM FALLS** into two different categories, "Modern Satanism" and "Traditional Satanism." Falling somewhere in between is a large variety of self-styled believers who may mix and match belief systems and practices.

We will begin with an examination of Modern Satanism.

**Modern Satanism** can trace its roots back to the "Satanic Bible" by Anton LaVey in the 1960s. Other veins of Modern Satanism include the Temple of Set founded in 1975 by Michael Aquino, and the First Church of Satan that follows the teachings of Aleister Crowley, a British occultist who lived from 1875–1947, over the teachings of LaVey. The philosophy of the Church of Satan started by Anton LaVey doesn't include personal Satan or devil. The belief system of Modern Satanism is essentially atheism, hedonism and self-worship. The creed of their belief is, "Do what thou wilt."

"Do what thou wilt" doesn't automatically make all Satanists law-breakers, deceivers, and baby killers. In fact, it's the goal of the Modern Satanist to become the best, and to achieve the best that life has to offer. If that means following the rules better than anyone else to get a better result than anyone else, then they will. However, if a Modern Satanist does decide to break a common law (speeding, for example), he does so because he chooses to. If he's caught, he's encouraged to matter of factly take consequences because of his choice. Generally, a Modern Satanist doesn't deny breaking the law; he simply admits to his choice, because it was what he would choose to do. ("Do what thou wilt.")

The Modern Satanists organize themselves into groups, just as churches and congregations do. These groups are called covens, grottoes, or pylons. Any group associated with the Church of Satan is headed by a priest. Any group associated with the Temple of Set is headed by a Grand Master. Unlike Christian churches or worship groups, they rarely meet for weekly gatherings of worship, but rather engage in rituals in order to dedicate themselves.

No one knows the exact number of satanic believers, as they tend to be secretive, and the requirements for membership are minimal—usually nothing more than desire.

As far as required observances, there are none for the Modern Satanist. Although being a religion of self-gratification, their most important holidays are their birthdays. Remember, this is a religion of hedonism, and they take their indulgences as seriously as religious duty.

Below you will find the **Nine Satanic Statements of the Church of Satan** and their code of conduct, **Rules of the Earth**. Both are found in *The Satanic Bible*. They'll give you much needed insight into how the modern Satanist thinks.

## Nine Satanic Statements

1. Satan represents indulgence, instead of abstinence!

2. Satan represents vital existence, instead of spiritual pipe dreams!

3. Satan represents undefiled wisdom, instead of hypocritical self-deceit!

4. Satan represents kindness to those who deserve it, instead of love wasted on ingrates!

5. Satan represents vengeance, instead of turning the other cheek!

6. Satan represents responsibility to the responsible, instead of concern for psychic vampires!

7. Satan represents man as just another animal, sometimes better, more often worse than those that walk on all fours, who because of his divine spiritual and intellectual development, has become the most vicious animal of all!

8. Satan represents all of the so-called sins, as they all lead to physical, mental, or emotional gratification.

9. Satan is the best friend the church has ever had, as he has kept it in business all these years!

## Rules of the Earth

1. Do not give opinions or advice unless you are asked.

2. Do not tell your troubles to others unless you are sure that they want to hear them.

3. When in another's lair, show him respect or else don't go there

4. If a guest in your lair annoys you, treat him cruelly and without mercy.

5. Do not make sexual advances unless you are given the mating signal.

6. Do not take that which doesn't belong to you unless it's a burden to the person and he cries out to be relieved.

7. Acknowledge the power of magick if you have used it successfully to obtain your desires. If you deny the power of magick after having called upon it with success, you will lose all you have obtained.

8. Do not complain about anything to which you need not subject yourself.

9. Do not harm little children.

10. Do not kill nonhuman animals unless attacked or for your food.

11. When walking in open territory, bother no one. If someone bothers you, ask him to stop. If he doesn't stop, destroy him.

Traditional Satanists (or devil worshippers) are a little harder to peg because they are eclectic in their practices—picking and choosing which writings inspire them. The major difference between them and the Modern Satanists is that these people believe in and worship a literal devil, and use his lesser deities to do their bidding. This Satan *can* be seen as the devil of the Christian Bible, but in most instances is viewed instead as a liberator of mankind, one who influences change and individuality. A good number of Traditional Satanists view the God of the Bible as an evil ruler, one who loves to punish, and Satan as the one who overcame Him. So, in speaking to either group, you may both be naming God and Satan, but your definitions of God and Satan may be diametrically opposed.

Into this category falls the Temple of Set. Members of the Temple of Set believe that they are worshipping in a truer form because they reject the trappings of the Church of Satan and embrace "The Prince of Darkness" with his Egyptian name, Set. They believe that a senior Initiate invoked The Prince of Darkness while looking for new orders in forming their breakaway sect. The orders were given by Satan, and put into a book entitled, "Coming Forth by Night." The Temple of Set was later incorporated in California and gained tax-exempt status as a religious organization.

Traditional Satanism is much less common than its younger brother, Modern Satanism, but Traditional Satanists are just as serious about their hedonism. They will participate actively in rituals regarding everything from baby dedication to the destruction of enemies.

There is a third, very small portion of Satanists referred to as "dabblers." Satanic dabblers are usually teenagers, who don't have a group affiliation. Dabblers are often obvious in their appearance. They will dress as dramatically as possible and usually have a Satanist symbol of some type on their clothing or person, such as a tattoo. I mention the appearance of a dabbler, because it stands in contrast to a Traditional or Modern Satanist, who prefers to blend into his or her environment, and will therefore present nothing distinctive in dress or style.

## Why are Satanists an "occult" group?

Satanists are classical occultists as defined by their need to know something hidden. Attempts to connect with the dark side require the use of rituals. Modern Satanism relies heavily on rituals that been written in large part by Anton LaVey and are very theatrical Rituals allow the Satanist to manipulate people, nature, and circumstances. (Ironically, the Modern Satanist claims to not believe in the spirit world.)

## What are some common lies within Satanism?

Satanism is Satanism, so lies really should not be so surprising. In fact, they are the norm. But let's take a look at a few. Let's start with Anton LaVey, who wrote "The Satanic Bible." Remember, an occultist loves to project an image of the person as whom he would like to be seen, and not as who he actually is. LaVey took the impressive name of Anton Szandor LaVey, hiding his real, but less exotic name, Howard Stanton Levey. According to LaVey, his Transylvanian Gypsy grandmother introduced him to the dark side. In reality, his grandmother was from the Ukraine and never introduced him to anything. His book, "The Satanic Bible," which he claimed to be the inspired work of Satan, was plagiarized from the writings of Ragnar Redbeard (circa 1896), and John Dee who wrote the "Enochian Keys," another plagiarism of Aleister Crowley's "Equinox." In other words, dear Anton wasn't exactly who he said that he was.

## What about Halloween?

There is a lot of misinformation concerning this holiday. Many assume that Halloween is one of the more important holidays in Satanism. Indeed, it's an important time to perform rituals, but specifically the history of this holiday is more of the Druidic Pagan nature. Although the Satanist might enter into a ritual on this evening, it will not necessarily involve human or animal sacrifice.

# Symbols of Satanism

**Pentagram** (Five-pointed star)

Inverted, it is one of the most easily recognizable symbols for Satan.

**Heartagram** (Pentagram and heart combined)

I included this symbol for clarification purposes. This is a symbol or logo for the 'Love Metal' band, HIM (His

Infernal Majesty). The name of the band implies an allegiance to Satan, and the logo combines the inverted pentagram with a heart. The combination of the Satanic pentagram and the heart denotes that there is a combination of love and hate/anger, or life and death. This symbol is worn as a tattoo by many of the fans of this band. Also, Bam Margera, 'Jackass' stuntman, wears the heartagram in a tattoo. This symbol is a popular cultural icon, but only because it's interesting. It doesn't necessarily denote involvement in Satanism.

**Goat of Mendes** (Mendez Goat)

Sigil (sign) of Bahomet, Sabbatic goat: Anton LaVey's Church of Satan uses a "simplified" version of this sigil as their logo. Without the goat, this is the inverted pentagram

## Alchemical Symbol for Sulfur

Identifying symbol for many Satanists.

# Chapter Fourteen

## Wicca and Witchcraft

**FROM *MACBETH* by** William Shakespeare (1564-1616)

*A dark cave. In the middle, a caldron boiling. Thunder. Enter the three* Witches.

1 WITCH. Thrice the brinded cat hath mew'd.

2 WITCH. Thrice and once, the hedge-pig whin'd.

3 WITCH. Harpier cries:—'tis time! 'tis time!

1 WITCH. Round about the caldron go;
    In the poison'd entrails throw. —
    Toad, that under cold stone,
    Days and nights has thirty-one;
    Swelter'd venom sleeping got,
    Boil thou first i' the charmed pot!
    ALL. Double, double toil and trouble;
    Fire burn, and caldron bubble.

2 WITCH. Fillet of a fenny snake,
    In the caldron boil and bake;
    Eye of newt, and toe of frog,
    Wool of bat, and tongue of dog,
    Adder's fork, and blind-worm's sting,

Lizard's leg, and owlet's wing,—
For a charm of powerful trouble,
Like a hell-broth boil and bubble.
ALL. Double, double toil and trouble;
Fire burn, and caldron bubble.

3 Witch. Scale of dragon; tooth of wolf;
Witches' mummy; maw and gulf
Of the ravin'd salt-sea shark;
Root of hemlock digg'd in the dark;
Liver of blaspheming Jew;
Gall of goat, and slips of yew
Sliver'd in the moon's eclipse;
Nose of Turk, and Tartar's lips;
Finger of birth-strangled babe
Ditch-deliver'd by a drab, —
Make the gruel thick and slab:
Add thereto a tiger's chaudron,
For the ingredients of our caldron.
ALL. Double, double toil and trouble;
Fire burn, and caldron bubble.

2 Witch. Cool it with a baboon's blood,
Then the charm is firm and good.


Witchcraft has been around for a long time. In fact, there are those who believe that it's the oldest religion on the planet. While this might be exaggerated, it's true that some practices have been handed down through many generations.

Wicca and Witchcraft are included here because of the common occultic thread that runs through them and all other forms of Paganism or occultism: The practice of magick, divination, and spiritism—the search for hidden things.

[*Point of clarification: Although Satanism, Wicca/ Witchcraft, and Neo-Paganism practice all three of these "arts," they are completely separate. They are practiced in very different ways, frequently in opposition to each other.*]

Although Wicca and Witchcraft vary widely in practice, generally they fall into two major categories.

## Wicca, White Witchcraft, or White Magick

Until recently, it's been very hard for anyone to find accurate information concerning Wicca. Just like other forms of occultism, this one prefers to keep its practices secret. As a result, Wicca has suffered from a number of misconceptions that have linked it with those who practice Black Witchcraft and Satanism.

Contrary to popular myth, Wiccans don't attack Christians, desecrate churches, or drink blood. Wicca is more of an earthy religion whose followers prefer to be known as "the wise ones." They revere nature and the "Natural Life Forces," which they believe everyone has. It's quite common for Wiccans to believe that the best place to find God is within yourself. Wiccans tend to reject the idea of the Christian "God, the Father." Instead, they worship the Life Forces, even designating them as male and female. Common monikers are the God and Goddess, Lord and Lady, and sometimes the Horned God (yes, he has horns, and no, you will not be able to convince them that he is the devil) and the Silver Lady. In this belief system, the female is the dominant force, bringing the Mother Earth concept into play. Actually, most Wiccans see Mother Earth as a real, live being. Wiccans are not into proselytizing, and prefer everyone to take their own path to eternity. And of course, they believe that all paths lead to the same place. It's very hard to convince a Wiccan that their practices are bad or wrong, because they are so involved in doing good or White Magick. Their rede states their strongest doctrine: "In that you harm none, do what thou wilt."

## Black Magick, or the Left Hand Path

Now, let's look at "the dark side"—the practitioners of Witchcraft or Black Magick.

As astonishing as this might sound, neither "White Light" nor "Black Magick" Witches tend to believe in a "personal" devil. They see him more as a dark force that comes from within the universe. Many Witches (not Wiccans) believe that they are tapping into a dark force, and call it the "Dark Way." Both Wiccans and those who practice this refer to it as "The Left Hand Path."

Unfortunately, this is the place where Witchcraft takes a decidedly nasty turn. Unlike Wiccans (sometimes referred to as "fluff bunnies" by this group), those who practice Black Magick seek power for selfish fulfillment. Many, if not most, of these people acknowledge that they are seeking power from a dark force or even from spirits, but don't acknowledge that this is evil. In fact, they don't believe in "good versus evil." So again, the way most Christians see things just doesn't apply. Yes, this force is dark. Yes, it's dangerous. But from their perspective, it's not evil. Even so, the views that come from those who engage with spirits associated with darkness range widely. Some Witches consider these forces, with their varied personalities, simply to be misunderstood. Other Witches consider these spirits downright dangerous. Those black Witches, who call on Lucifer or any other dark spirit, are more concerned with doing a "business transaction" than with actually worshipping them.

## Similarities between Wicca and Black Witchcraft

These two practices are sometimes confused with each other because of things they share in common. To the casual observer who notices the similarities, the lines between Wicca and Black Witchcraft can become blurred, if not obliterated altogether. Both have practitioners who might meet in groups of thirteen people. The groups are called covens, although today, covens represent the minority.

They both believe that through certain rituals or ceremonies, they can predict the future or communicate with loved ones who have passed.

They both tend to believe in reincarnation, although they don't believe that they might come back as animals. They think they continue to "recycle" until they make it to a version of heaven.

And they all believe that they can, by ritual or ceremony, manipulate and influence circumstances, nature, and people. To a Wiccan, however, it's taboo to even think of manipulating a person without consent.

## Differences between Wicca and Black Witchcraft

From a Christian point of view, it's tricky to make distinctions and see the differences between these groups. However, we can't stress enough how important it is for you to be able to tell them apart. Remember, Wiccans firmly believe that they are seeking truth and light. They are drawn to spirits that are friendly and helpful. Black Witches are drawn to spirits that are evil or dark because they are looking for a personal source of selfish power. This thinking would repulse a Wiccan.

# Interview with a Former Witch

In 2004, we had the privilege of watching a practitioner of The Craft (or Black Magick) come to know Jesus as Lord and Savior. Her name is Annie and she graciously agreed to answer several questions that many Christians have asked us about the dark practices. She's an expert.

**Jeff**: What was your first clue that you were being drawn into an occultic lifestyle?

**Annie**: My first clue was the fact that I could see and sense spirits. I didn't attach the term "occult" to them, but my curiosity about that sort of thing led me into the occult.

**Jeff**: How long were you involved?

**Annie**: I was seriously involved for seven years. For about three years before that, I had only dabbled.

**Jeff**: In your opinion, do Witches (not Wiccans) have any idea that they are serving demons?

**Annie**: I can't speak for all of them, but in my case, I knew that the entities that I invoked were not always pleasant, and could be downright dangerous.

**Jeff**: Did your parents know? And if so how much did they know?

**Annie**: My mother knew that I read some books about spirits and such, but had no idea how deep my interest went. So, I would have to say that she didn't know. I did my best to keep her from knowing about my activity.

**Jeff**: In your opinion, what signs or signals should a person look for if they suspect that their loved one has become involved in Wicca or Witchcraft?

**Annie**: Obviously, the craft is very secretive. So, anyone who is getting involved will become more withdrawn. Teenagers have the tendency to adopt a Gothic clothing style and express interest in the paranormal. With adults, it's a bit harder to detect. Any sudden behavior changes should be noticed, but the person just as easily could be dealing with an addiction or some other issue totally unrelated to Witchcraft.

**Jeff**: What advice would you give to someone who has a loved one who's involved?

**Annie**: Prayer is the most powerful tool that we have. Pray that God will show them their need for Him. Don't exclude them from your life, or end the friendship or relationship. Through you, Christ can show them His love. There is no need to try to shove religion down their throats and attempt to convince them of anything. Your day-to-day walk with God will draw their attention more than anything you say.

# Examples of Ceremonial Tools and Symbols

### Atheme
A knife, which is generally not used for cutting. Most of the time it's used to direct energy "flowing" from a spell.

### Broom
No, witches don't fly; they use their brooms for symbolic purification (cleaning) and protection.

## Cauldron

Basically, a big pot cast out of various kinds of metal (iron, brass), and used to create potions. Frequently symbolizes the goddess.

## Pentacle

A pentagram in a circle. Sometimes mistaken as the satanic pentagram (which is inverted). It's seen as one of the most powerful tools of protection and summoning.

## Elven Star

Used by practitioners of Faery Traditions.

## Wand

A handheld stick used to invoke spirits or deities. The kind of wood used in each wand is important; different woods perform different tasks.

# Wiccan Holidays

### Samhain (Halloween) - October 31

Samhein is the Wiccan New Year, and is one of the four major holidays of Wicca. At this time, the god passes into the otherworld to be reborn to the goddess of Yule. The division between the worlds is thin, and it is a time to remember one's ancestors and to reflect on the past year. In the past, animals were slaughtered for food during the winter and the tribal chief took part in the ritual as the king stag.

### Yule (Winter Solstice) - circa December 20-23

Yule is a time of rebirth and renewal. At Yule, the goddess gives birth to her son, the god who is symbolized by the sun. His birth brings hope and the promise of the coming summer. Yule is a remnant of older rituals, which hurried the end of winter and the coming of spring.

### Imbolc (Brigid, Candlemas) - February 2

Imbolc is one of the four major holidays of Wicca. Imbolc marks the growth of the god into a strong boy, as the days grow longer and the sun gets stronger. It also marks the recovery of the goddess from giving birth to the god. It is a time of initiation, a beginning, as the seeds begin to wake from their winter sleep. Traditionally many initiation and self-dedication rituals are performed at this time.

### Ostara (Easter, Spring Equinox) - circa March 20-23

The Spring Equinox marks the first day of spring, when the god grows to maturity. The night and day are equal; therefore, it is a time of balance when our lives can be brought into harmony. It is a time of beginnings of action.

### Beltane (May Eve) - April 30

Beltane is one of the four major holidays of Wicca. Beltane is the emergence of the god into manhood. He falls in love with the goddess, and their union results in the goddess being with child. Beltane is the celebration of their coupling and the fertility of the earth goddess and all living things. Beltane marks the return of vitality and passion.

### Litha (Summer Solstice, Midsummer) - circa June 20-23

Midsummer falls on the longest day of the year. On this day, the god begins his journey toward death as the days begin to get shorter. In the past, bonfires were lit to encourage fertility, health, and love.

### Lammas (Lughnasadh) - August 1

Lammas is one of the four major holidays of Wicca. Lammas is the celebration of the successful growing season. The grain is ripe, but it is just beginning to be harvested. The god loses strength as the days grow shorter. It is time to address and overcome fears and anxiety.

### Mabon (Autumn Equinox) - circa September 20-23

Mabon is the celebration of a successful harvest. Once again, night and day are equal. It is a time to address the balance in our lives and to be thankful for success. The god continues to fade with the sun, while the goddess mourns his loss, but rejoices in her pregnancy.

# "Christian" Wicca

Believe it or not, yes, there are growing numbers of people who claim to be Wiccan *and* Christian. This group believes in the same things (understanding the many and various beliefs within Wicca) that most Wiccans do. The exception is that when they pray, they pray to God, the Holy Spirit, and Jesus. They don't believe that Christianity is the only way to God or that Christianity was intended to be a "rule bound" religion. They also enjoy reading Scriptures and applying their own interpretations. A good example is the common practice of wanting to use only the Gospels, and believing that Jesus spent a lot of time correcting outdated Scripture and laws (The Old Testament). Also, many Christian Wiccans interpret the Pauline epistles (and any other aspect deemed not acceptable) as the opinion of a mere man, not the inspired Word of God.

It's common for a Christian Wiccan to see God in many different ways. Sometimes, they see Him in two parts instead of a Trinity, Jesus representing the male part of God and the Holy Spirit, the female. The two combined are seen as Divinity. Some will actually claim a Trinity, but not the Christian Father, Son, and Holy Spirit. Instead, the Trinity is interpreted to be God, Goddess, and Jesus. Interestingly, one belief among Christian Wiccans is that Jesus Christ is coming back one day, although no one knows when.

# Chapter Fifteen

# Neo-Paganism

**ASK TWELVE PAGANS** to define Paganism, and you will end up with thirteen answers! It's true!

Simply put, Paganism is a polytheistic religion that rejects all monotheistic religions such as Christianity, Judaism and Islam. *[Polytheism is the belief or worship of more than one god.]* This definition encompasses a pretty broad category, into which fall most occultic religions except Modern and Traditional Satanism. (Because we've already covered Wicca and Witchcraft, for the sake of efficiency, we'll eliminate them from this section.)

A *Neo*-Pagan is anyone who falls into the above category, and who is trying to or has revived the practices of ancient polytheistic cultures. This includes, but is not limited to Druids (Celtic revival), Shamanism, Egyptian and Greek Revivalists, individuals who participate in Native American spirituality (Cherokee, Aztec, for example), Vodou, Palo Malombe, Santeria, and Far Eastern Spirituality. Because of the vastness of these topics, we've only chosen a few of the most common to examine.

The amazing thing about Neo-Paganism is that it's increasingly popular with well educated Baby Boomers and Generation X'rs. This group has made great strides toward tolerance and acceptance even among Christians. And if we followed blindly, we would soon believe as they do: that Christianity is just another "way."

# Druids (Celtic Revival)

The origins of Celtic Druidry reach back to ancient Britain, Ireland, and Scotland when they were invaded by the Celts during the first millennium. The Druids of ancient Britannia were the priests and philosophers for the people of their era. We know very little about them; apparently, it was forbidden to write down any of their teachings. They passed their knowledge on through oral presentation (word of mouth). Irish and Welsh monks preserved some of it in writing later.

Rumor suggests that Druids supervised human sacrifices, but only one archeological site has been found that actually pertains to sacrifice, and there was nothing found to prove whether or not this place was actually used for human sacrifice. Mostly because of the Roman Empire, and later the Christian Church, they were essentially extinct by 750 AD.

Around the 1200s, interest in the Druid way of life began to resurface in Britain. Later, William Stukelek (1629-1697) stirred up quite a bit of interest when he began the first serious study of Stonehenge since before the Middle Ages. Since then, the Druid tradition has been growing, evolving even until today. It has stretched well beyond the borders of Great Britain, and can be found in various forms all across the globe. The advent of the modern Paganism that began in the 1960s has had an adverse effect on the integrity of their original beliefs and practices. Indeed, traditional British Druidry has now been overshadowed by offshoots and modernized versions of this ancient Pagan religion.

Traditional Druids, along with Modern Druids, don't adhere to any particular creed. The Traditional Druids, while believing that all paths eventually lead to the same place, have no problem with the concept of one divine creator. Modern Druids, on the other hand, adhere to a more polytheistic and goddess-oriented way of thinking. Traditional Druids and some Modern Druids believe in an arduously long version of reincarnation, where an individual leaves Annwn (the primal cauldron of form), and must live through every stage of life from microorganism to plant to bug to animal, and finally, to human. At the human phase, they have the chance to make the jump to Gwynfydd (their version of heaven or enlightened life), or start all over at the microorganism stage. Other Druids simply believe in an afterlife much like the life we are living here. All groups see nature and life as holy. Because of this, Druids tend to have a deep reverence for all life forms.

Druids meet in different ways: sometimes going solo, sometimes worshipping in groups. Usually, when they do meet, it's in a grove of trees. Their code of conduct includes courage, honesty, and fairness. They also proclaim peace to the "four quarters" of the earth before most Druid ceremonies. Other than that, they are free to live as they please. They practice their own form of divination, using their alphabet Ogham, and perform rituals and ceremonies according to the occasion or the time of year.

The practice of Druidism is on the increase, with the former Archbishop of Canterbury in Britain recently accepting an official (if not honorary) position within the organization there. As romantically historical as they might be, Druids are occultists, not Christians.

## Symbols of Druidry

The most common Druid symbols are Ogham letters and a Tree of Life with outspread branches, sometimes in a Celtic knot design.

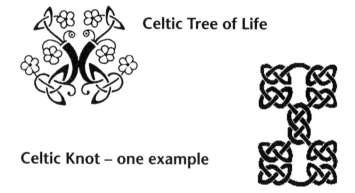

**Celtic Tree of Life**

**Celtic Knot – one example**

## Ogham (pronounced "AHG-m") Alphabet

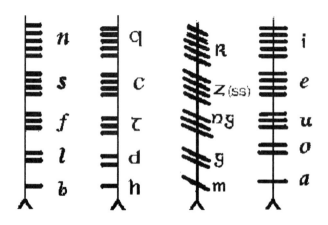

# Shamanism

The word "Shaman" comes from an ancient Siberian tribe called Tungus. Interestingly, Shamanism (though called by other names) is found within the history of every culture of hunters and gatherers that has ever lived.

A Shaman is a person who communicates with the dead, gathers information in dream states or trances, controls spirits, heals, and makes changes in the spirit world that influence the physical plain.

There are typically three ways to become a Shaman:

1. Heritage—the skill can be passed along through family, for example, from father to son or mother to daughter.

2. Calling—a person is called to Shamanism through a near death experience either physically or in dream state.

3. Personal choice or quest—a person decides to take this path. The person who becomes a Shaman by choice is considered to be less powerful.

Regardless of the path, a Shaman is not recognized as legitimate unless he or she has undergone training in dreams and trances (called "Ecstasy"), and techniques, knowledge of spirits (often represented by animals such as wolves and cougars), mythology and genealogy. The trances allow the individual to leave the body and seek communication with and control spirits, gain information, help dead souls, and make changes in the spirit world that will affect the physical world. "Ecstasy" comes from the Greek word *ekstasis*, and means, "to be placed outside." This is the literal pulling of the Shaman by a "spirit guide" or "god" outside of the body. This purpose of this can range from help in a given situation to prophetic utterance through the body of the Shaman.

# Native American Religion

Native American Religion has no founder, no formula and no two ways of practicing that are alike. The traditions are as varied as the many Native American tribes that once roamed the North American continent. The most common spiritual experience among the tribes is the "Vision Quest." This is a search for personal vision, sometimes led by priests or Shamans. Sometimes, the person on the Vision Quest seeks individual experiences with Spirit. In these quests, an individual goes out alone into the wilderness or desert for a number of days in search of spiritual power and a vision for his life or the life of the tribe. In some groups, the Vision Quest is a rite of passage into adulthood in which a young person seeks his or her lifelong spirit guide (often in the form of an animal). In other groups, the quest takes place at any time that a person needs guidance; sometimes this is practiced as personal discipline. In the past, the quest held great significance to young men who were training to be warriors.

All Native American groups enjoyed rituals and tribal gatherings and ceremonies. Every tribe has unique ways of celebrating. Sometimes these rituals are elaborate and sometimes extremely simple. They take place at different times of the year, often to purify the people, spiritually clean their homes, and make offerings. Native American groups also share a deep reverence for the world around them, even taking special care to perform the exact rituals in order to honor the spirits of the animals that they had killed.

Recently, there has been growing interest in Native American practices. The interesting part of this is that serious study of Native American culture didn't begin until the mid- to late 19th century. By that time, a number of Native Americans had converted to Christianity and forgotten their heritage, or had become extinct altogether. The Native Americans who *did* remember vowed not to share their knowledge with the white man. A quote regarding this attitude from the Lakota tribe goes something like this: "If it was told to a white man, it's untrue."

## Symbols of Native American Religion

### Kokopelli (wooden-backed)

This little god is depicted with a hunched back, dancing and playing the flute. His origins are ancient Native American. He can be found in various prehistoric rock carvings and drawings. Kokopelli is believed to have been a fertility symbol and is sometimes depicted carrying a bag of seeds. He is associated with rain, prosperity, marriage, pregnancy, and luck.

### Zia (sun)

Zia means "sun," and is also the name of this Pueblo sun symbol. It's the embodiment of the number four, representative of the powers of nature: the sun, the four directions (north, south, east, west), the seasons (winter, spring, summer, fall), and the ages of man. This symbol is the centerpiece of the state flag of New Mexico.

# Vodou, Vodoun, Vodun, or Voodoo

Vodou is the traditional religion of Haiti. The Vodou culture has its roots in African Spirituality. The main vein of Vodou started in Haiti, where large portions of Africans were brought into slavery and forced into Christianity. (This is a prime example of just *WHY* a person cannot force anyone to accept Christ.) Vodou is a mixture of the occultic beliefs of many different African tribes with a smattering of Christian beliefs mixed in for good measure.

Vodou is a group or family effort; no one does this alone. Even initiation is only done through a strong leader: "Mama" or "Papa," because of the apparent danger.

According to African tradition, there is one god, Bondje, who is distant from all that he has created. So, instead of going to Bondje for help, requests are given to spirit helpers, ancestors or even Catholic saints. As a matter of fact, it's quite common to see pictures of Catholic saints as representative of these helpers. Vodou "helpers" are neither good nor evil. They tend to conduct themselves in a very "human" manner: needing to be appeased with sacrifices or offerings in order to keep them from getting angry. These spirits are divided according to their nature. Hot spirits are most commonly from Haiti; cool spirits are from Africa. They run in families. It's important to note that as in other Pagan traditions, there is no strict and singular way to practice Vodou. Different spirits are the heads of different (spiritual) families, and the natures of those families are reflected in the spirits that lead them. Every practice is dictated to the next generation by the "Mama" or "Papa," and can be as different and varied as the colors of the rainbow.

Vodou is practiced in two traditions. Obeah (folk magic), sometimes also referred to as Hoodoo, is practiced in Haiti. It's gaining popularity in the Creole states such as Louisiana and lower Alabama. The other tradition is the worship of Loa, which originated in Africa. The primary goal of this form of worship is to "entice" specific deities or ancestors to inhabit or possess the bodies of worshipers in order to speak through them.

The amazing thing that we found regarding this religion is that in all of our research, we kept coming across statements like, " Vodou is one of the most misunderstood and misrepresented religions of all time;" and "The evil picture that everyone has of Vodou can be blamed on Hollywood." However, after delving into credible sources of information, it quickly became clear that although a large portion of Vodou magic is practiced to gain wealth or good fortune, there is also a great deal of time spent cursing enemies, sometimes with the intent to kill.

## Symbols of Vodou

### Verve
This decorative symbol is drawn to entice a deity to come to an individual. Each deity has its own unique symbols.

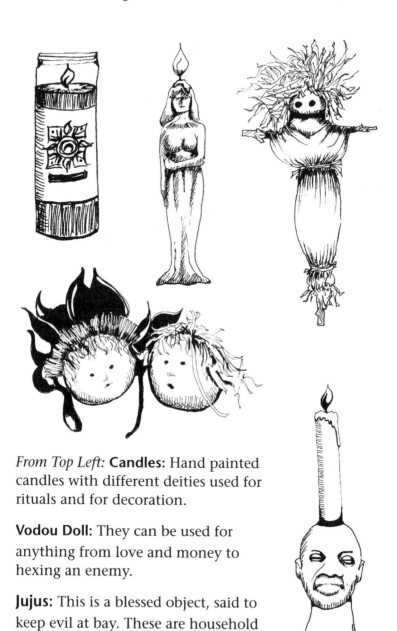

*From Top Left:* **Candles:** Hand painted candles with different deities used for rituals and for decoration.

**Vodou Doll:** They can be used for anything from love and money to hexing an enemy.

**Jujus:** This is a blessed object, said to keep evil at bay. These are household spirits.

**Papa Ellegua** is said to give assistance when a person is at a crossroad.

# Santeria, La Regla Lucumi
## (The Way of the Saints)

Santeria is the Cuban brother to Vodou. Like Vodou, it began with slaves from Africa and is hidden among island practitioners of the Catholic faith. In the United States today, it is most prevalent in south Florida, where Cubans have settled. In fact, the animal protection laws in Miami and the surrounding counties have had to be modified to allow ritualistic animal sacrifice so that practitioners may worship without religious persecution.

Santeria is a blended faith. When the slaves arrived in Cuba, they were given two choices: Become a Catholic and eat, or don't become a Catholic and starve. The choice was obvious. Because these slaves could relate to the abused Son of God, they had no problem worshipping him in the Catholic Church. However, they practiced polytheistic religions before they converted. So they simply added Jesus to the group of deities that they already worshiped. They hid the old familiar gods by disguising them with the names of Catholic saints. This way, they could actually sit in a Catholic worship service and yet be worshipping the deity of their choice. In fact, because practitioners use Catholic articles of worship, Santeria can be a little hard to identify.

As a person digs a little deeper, though, Santeria is just as grotesque as Vodou. Santerians worship their chosen deity, the Orisha (or Saint). But the concept of "choice" turns sinister when one considers that, in fact, the Orisha chooses the worshiper. This mutual choice defines a relationship, the ultimate goal of which is for the devotee to become the "possession," or even better, the lover of the particular deity. Each deity has a favorite day of the week, and a favorite food and color. In ceremonies of worship, devotees wear the color related to the particular deity, and a beaded necklace. Practices include using potions, sacrificing animals, and drinking animal blood. Small, personal shrines filled with trinkets are common.

# Kabbalah

Fascination with the Kabbalah is the sudden new "thing to do" in Hollywood and other trendy circles. According to Rabbi Shimon Leiberman, this popular form of Kabbalah is nothing more than "incomprehensible mumbo-jumbo and a smorgasbord of pop psychology." Even the fashionable and popular red string bracelet (often sold for $25.00 per string) is nonsense.

The Kabbalah was developed among the Jews while they were in Babylon. The word Kabbalah or Cabala means, "to receive." It's not a religion, but as Rabbi Leiberman says, " Kabbalah is to Torah what philosophy is to science."

This Jewish philosophy concentrates deeply on the nature of God and His true essence in an effort to know Him better through the "Ten Sefirot" or ten qualities or essences of God. These Ten Sefirot are not themselves little, individual gods, but different aspects of the nature or personality of God. They are depicted in the Tree of Life, and consist of, in descending order, Keter (the crown), Chokhmah (wisdom), Binah (intuition, understanding), Chesed (mercy) or Gedulah (greatness), Gevurah (strength), Tiferet (glory), Netzach (victory), Hod (majesty), Yesod (foundation) and Malkut (sovereignty). The middle five qualities are mentioned explicitly and in order in 1 Chronicles 29:11:

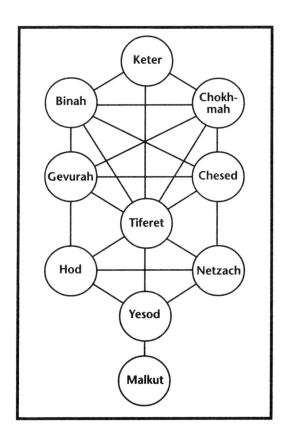

*"Yours, O L-rd, is the greatness (gedulah), the strength (gevurah), the glory (tiferet), the power (netzach), and the splendor (hod)."*

If the Kabbalah stuck only to philosophy, it could be dismissed as Jewish pondering the nature of God. However, practicality is where the Kabbalah dips itself into the occult with numerology (predictions found in number patterns), talismans (objects that protect or have divine powers), and amulets (symbols worn for protection or purpose). And consistent with the definition of the occult, Kabbalah teaches that one can find hidden meaning in numerical and alphabetical interpretation of Old Testament texts.

The "Hollywood" version of Kabbalah sounds more like a cross between Wicca and New Age with Jewish symbols and verbiage thrown in for color and flavor. There's a lot of talk about attaining a new level of "light," inner personal freedom, and the "divine" in all of us. This popular version of Kabbalah is also called Universal Kabbalah, and is paired with Kundalini Yoga (a New Age form of Transcendental Meditation). This is simply a reinvented version of man's age-old quest that began in the Garden: to become like God. The deceptive attraction of this trap is that proponents of Kabbalah actually refer to God as the source of light. This seems harmless enough until you are a few pages into the study and realize that the purpose in seeking God is not to worship Him or obey Him, but to be Him ... to be as God.

> "That sunlight emanates from the Creator of our universe. We can follow it to its source, and when we do, we discover our own source. When we do, instead of praying to God, obeying God, fearing God, or rejecting God, we become like God." – Michael Berg in an open letter regarding his book, *Becoming like God, Kabbalah and our Ultimate Destiny*

Hmmmm ... it seems like we've heard this lie once before in a certain Garden ... Genesis, Chapter 3.

Rabbis and true Jewish Kabbalahists look on these new practices with great disdain, stating that Tarot card readings, divination, and other forms of magick are *not* a part of the original Kabbalah. They have nicknamed this form of Kabbalah, "crap-bala," and warn that the symbols used by its practitioners, such as their own interpretations of the Tree of Life, are being used out of context, and are wrong and offensive.

# Chapter Sixteen

## Vampires and Goths

**INTEREST IN VAMPIRISM** has had a romantic resurgence in recent years thanks in great part to a number of popular television series, movies and books. Anyone who has any knowledge of vampire lore has heard of Bram Stoker's *Dracula*. Not many know that this book is based on the real life of Vlad Tepes Dracula, a gruesome, blood-lusting ruler from the fifteenth century. Vampirism has long held a literary and cinematic fascination, because of the subliminal sexual themes of people feeding off each other. If you'll note, vampires are always depicted as tragic, sensual creatures, who wander the night in search of companions. Their plight and lifestyle can be highly attractive to young people with vivid imaginations and black wardrobes. There's even a popular series of books published by Cirque Du Freak and marketed to young girls, ages 11-14. The series promotes itself as "a perfect book for the reluctant middle school reader. For those fans of Buffy and Angel, here is another book to satisfy their vampiric tastes."

Vampirism in itself is not a religion. It would be accurate to say that a person can be a Satanist and a vampire, but not all vampires are Satanists, nor are all

Satanists, vampires. The same applies to vampirism and any other type of Paganism.

Vampires come in three varieties: those who drink blood, those who feed on energy and refer to themselves as Psychic Vampires, and those who do both. No matter what the practice, the purpose of vampirism is to drain energy or vitality or "life force" (contained in its strongest form in blood) from a person.

**Count Vlad Tepes Dracula**

The blood-drinking vampires are self-explanatory. No, they are not the Hollywoodized "un-dead" who roam the night and vaporize when sunlight hits them or someone flashes a crucifix. Garlic doesn't send them screaming back to the crypt. They're merely people. Most often, these blood-drinkers will drink their own blood or share that of others who also participate in this practice. They usually don't drink much—just a taste, and the blood they drink is drawn through bites, cuts, or a needle and syringe.

A Psychic Vampire enhances his or her life force by draining it away from an unaware, hapless victim. This is done mainly through visualization. A Psychic Vampire sees a person's energy field, and simply visualizes it "flowing" from the victim into himself. This supposedly energizes and invigorates the Vampire, and leaves the "victim" feeling drained.

# Goths

The Goth scene had its beginnings in the very late 1970s and early 1980s. The term Goth is said to have come from a little known band in 1979 by the name of Bauhaus and their release of a song, "Bela Lugosi's Dead." In its infancy, Goth was viewed as a subclassification of punk, but soon was strong enough of a movement to stand alone.

Like vampirism, Goth is not a religion. The foundation of the Gothic philosophy is, in a nutshell, depression. We have found kids from every walk of life, from Satanists to Born Again Christians (really ... no, really!) who have become involved in this widespread subculture.

The Gothic culture is one steeped in the dark side of life. Often the participants have a romantic fascination with death and dying. Goths celebrate "the beauty of pain" with nods to forbidden love and deep, profound sorrow. A distinguishing characteristic of the Goths is their dress. They clothe themselves as though they have come out of the Middle Ages or off the movie set of "The Crow" or "Van Helsing." Goth kids often wear velvet dresses of dark rich color or dress head-to-toe in black, black and purple, black and crimson, or any other dark combination. Some will dye their hair black or a stark, vivid color. Some will wear heavy makeup that emphasizes a pale face with dramatic eye and lip color. Some sport tattoos and piercings. Some wear contact lenses designed to shock. This distinctive styling was perfected by "Club Kids," and made instantly recognizable through media. We have found that in **most** cases, the outfit or ensemble worn on the outside is almost a mirror image of what is happening on the inside: darkness.

On the whole, the Gothic culture has a philosophy of acceptance and tolerance. Because Goth is not a religion, they have a wide range of beliefs: Agnostic, Jewish, Satanic, Wiccan, Christian, and anything else you can think of. Their practices range just as widely. One advantage you'll have in rescuing a loved one from the Gothic culture is that they tend to be accessible. They're not particularly secretive or exclusionary. Goths have no problem hanging out with anyone as long as they are treated with respect. Liz and I move freely though Gothic groups, and although we certainly don't dress "Goth," we've been made more than welcome. And as ironic as this might sound coming from a group made distinctive by their dark dress and morose presence, they don't like being stereotyped. Individually, you'll find many to be intelligent with wonderful senses of humor.

The term "Christian Goth" at first glance seems to be an oxymoron. But on further examination, this is a very positive progression for an individual who is seeking peace and some understanding of the sad world in which we live. This group is learning to come to terms with the fact that we live on a planet that's under a curse.

Christian Goths are often instrumental in leading others to Christ. One of our favorite Christian web sites, www.ChristianGoth.com, uses a very powerful Scripture found in Isaiah to proclaim their faith:

> *The people who walked in darkness have seen a great light; Those who dwelt in the land of the shadow of death, upon them a light has shined"* (Isaiah 9:2).

If you have a loved one who is involved in the Gothic culture, don't automatically assume that he or she is a

Satanist or Wiccan/Witch. Black clothes are not indicative of core belief. As I've said, they're indicative of depression.

With Goths, the best thing to do is to simply love them and participate in their lives. Watch the movies and listen to their music with them. This way you'll begin to understand what they are feeling, but are not quite able to express fully. If they are Christians, offer to participate as much as possible in their lives, invite their friends to dinner, encourage their Bible study, and ask for their opinions. Because Goths are not exclusionary, it should be fairly easy to move in closely and stay there, where you can make sure depression doesn't go too far or last too long, and keep their potential in focus for that moment when they're ready to move on from Goth to real life. We have yet to see anyone from *any* culture that isn't moved by genuine care and love.

# Part Three

# How to rescue someone you love from the occult

# Chapter Seventeen

# Making Help Available—Rescue

**WHEN THE TIME COMES** to rescue someone, we often get called. We're summoned for two reasons. First, the callers want to rely on our experience and confidence. Second, and more significant, they're afraid to attempt a rescue alone.

"What if something goes wrong? What if the demons are too strong? What if something tries to hurt me? What if I become possessed? What if I am followed home by an evil entity? What if I enrage Satan? What if I die?"

Put all doubts aside. Don't be afraid. The bad news is that you can't rescue anyone. The good news is that God can … and He is going to use you to get the job done. There is very little that you need to know and very little you need to do. Your responsibility is to show up and follow His instructions.

We'll show you that not only are you more than equal to the task, but you're fully protected. Nothing will harm you as you march into battle in the full armor of God.

Here's how to make sure you're fully equipped.

## Represent Jesus

Before you can help ANYONE coming out of ANYTHING, especially those trapped in the occult, make certain that you are a true representative of Jesus Christ. How do you know you are?

You must be a born again Christian. In the Book of John, Jesus said, "Most assuredly, I say to you, unless one is born again, he cannot see the kingdom of God" (John 3:3 NKJV). From our experience, many very nice people attend church and some have even taught Sunday school for years, but are not born again. When facing anything pertaining to the occult, being a "good person who goes to church" isn't enough. You must be absolutely sure of your relationship with God, and this assurance comes in being born again.

The Book of Acts tells of the sons of Sceva, who ran into all sorts of problems when they tried to confront the demonic without knowing Jesus as their Lord and Savior. The story begins with the miracles that God was performing through the hands of Paul:

> *So that even handkerchiefs or aprons were brought from his (Paul's) body to the sick and the diseases left them and the evil spirits went out of them.*

> *Then some of the itinerant Jewish exorcists took it upon themselves to call the name of the Lord Jesus over those who had evil spirits, saying, "We adjure you by the Jesus whom Paul preaches."*

> *Also there were seven sons of Sceva, a Jewish chief priest, who did so.*

*And the evil spirit answered and said, "Jesus I know, and Paul I know; but who are you?*

*Then the man in whom the evil spirit was leaped on them, overpowered them, and prevailed against them, so that they fled out of that house naked and wounded" (Acts 19:11 -16 NKJV).*

So exactly how is one born again? First, you need to understand that God loves you and has a wonderful plan for your life.

*"God so loved the world that He gave His one and only Son, that whoever believes in Him shall not perish, but have eternal life." (John 3:16 NIV)*

*"I came that they might have life, and might have it abundantly" (John 10:10 NIV)*

Next, you need to remember that man is sinful, and our sin has separated us from God. By ourselves, there is NO WAY that we can know and experience God's love and plan for us.

*"All have sinned and fall short of the glory of God" (Romans 3:23).*

Man was created to have fellowship with God, but because of his stubborn self-will, he chose to believe that independence from God was better than dependence. This has never been more evident than today. Active rebellion and passive indifference characterize the choices people make. Just look at the world around us; people are either proud of their lifestyles (have you ever watched the MTV awards?) or they don't want to be bothered to change themselves or anyone around them. In other words, "If there is a God, He would love me just the way I am. Why should I change?" These actions and attitudes are indications of sin. Sin separates us from God.

*"The wages of sin is death" (Romans 5:23).*

We need to understand that there are ONLY two ways to pay these "wages." We can suffer death ourselves. (By choosing to be independent from God, we **choose** eternity without God in hell.) Or we can accept the gift that He gives us.

*"God demonstrates His own love toward us, in that while we were yet sinners, Christ died for us" (Romans 5:8 NIV).*

In other words, when Jesus died on the cross, He voluntarily paid our "wages" for us. Once our debt was paid, the curse of death was no longer in effect. This was confirmed when Jesus rose from the grave.

It's very common to hear that "there are many paths to God." Wrong. If we truly are Christians, then we understand that Jesus meant what He said:

*"I am the way, the truth, and the life; no one comes to the Father, but through Me" (John 14:5 NIV).*

Finally, we must individually receive Jesus Christ as our Savior and as Lord of our lives. This means that we accept Him, commit to Him, and are devoted to Him over ourselves.

*"As many as received Him, to them He gave the right to become children of God, even to those who believe in His name" (John 1:12 NKJV).*

We need to understand that there is NOTHING we can do to attain salvation other than accepting His gift. We simply believe. This is faith. This faith is not the kind that believes in Santa or the Easter Bunny. It's practical and useful. It's demonstrated when you sit in your favorite chair and assume that it will hold you up without collapsing ... and it does. Or when you go to bed at night and assume that the sun will rise in the morning ... and it does. Faith in God is as real as that. You can count on Him to respond to you ... and He does. Just believe.

The best way to acknowledge your belief in Him is to pray. If you would like to ask Jesus to become the Lord of your life, you are welcome to pray this prayer with us right now. Just make sure that you mean what you pray. Don't ever "just repeat" anything; it's pointless. If you have an active relationship with Him and would like to renew your commitment, this would be a good time to do it. Don't wait until tomorrow. Please pray something like this:

> "Lord Jesus, I need You. Thank You for dying on the cross for my sins. Please forgive my independence from You. I'm now choosing to be dependent on You. I'm choosing You as my Lord and Savior, and ask You now to take charge of my life. Thank You for forgiving me. Please make me the kind of person that You want me to be. In Jesus' name I pray. Amen."

If you just prayed this prayer, we welcome you to our family in Christ.

## Put yourself aside, and represent Jesus Christ in all that you do and say.

As we said earlier, you need to be certain that you're a representative of Jesus Christ before you march into the occult with a life preserver. If you are a true representative, then you know that Jesus accepts people while they're still sinners, and so will you. As a matter of fact, Jesus was well known for going into the homes of sinners, where He loved and accepted them. Through His kindness, sinners repented.

> *"You, therefore, have no excuse, you who pass judgment on someone else, for at whatever point you judge the other, you are condemning yourself, because you who pass judgment do the same things. Now we know that God's judgment against those who do such things is based on truth, so when you, a mere man, pass judgment on them and yet do the same things, do you think you will escape God's judgment?" (Romans 2:1-3 NIV).*

When Romans refers to our judging others while sinning ourselves, the passage defines our common sin as basic rebellion. When we judge others, we decide that they're wrong. We're right. When we do this, we take God's authority into our own hands ... and at the very least, try to change people before they are ready. Whenever we act apart from God, we are in rebellion. And by the way, 1 Samuel 15:23 states, "For rebellion is as the sin of witchcraft, and stubbornness is as iniquity and idolatry" (NKJV). So, when we rebel and act outside of what and how and when God wants to do something, we are guilty of sin that, according to God, falls into the same category as witchcraft and idolatry. We are just as guilty as they are.

Jesus never forced anyone to repent of sin. His love and compassion were sufficient for people to want to repent. Remember that we've ALL sinned and fallen short of His glory. We have no right to think that ANYONE is inferior to us because they are in sin. We are redeemed; they are in need of redemption. If our judgment makes it impossible for God to use us for another person's redemption, then we are in rebellion and pride. And just in case you haven't read Proverbs lately, "Pride goes before destruction" (Proverbs 16:18).

Now, let's take a look at the kindness of God, and how we can be a reflection of Him so that others will be drawn to Him and not us.

*"Or do you show contempt for the riches of His kindness, tolerance and patience, not realizing that God's kindness leads you towards repentance?" (Romans 2:4, NIV).*

I think the best description of the character of God comes from God Himself in Exodus 34. At Moses' request, the Lord God revealed His glory. God did this by passing in front of Moses and covering his eyes with His hand so that Moses couldn't see His face, but could see His glory after The Lord had passed. When The Lord did this, He proclaimed:

*"The Lord, The compassionate and gracious God, slow to anger, abounding in love and faithfulness, maintaining love to thousands, and forgiving wickedness, rebellion, and sin. Yet He doesn't leave the guilty unpunished: He punishes the children and their children for the sin of the fathers to the third and fourth generation" (Exodus 34:6,7).*

As you see, God is about justice. But, He is also about compassion, graciousness, mercy, love, faithfulness, and forgiveness. In God's qualities, we see a template for our own behavior. In order for justice and judgment to be true and real, they need to be God's justice and judgment, not ours.

Of course, this is easier said than done, but there's no better place to put the principles into practice than when you're faced with a loved one caught in the bondage of the occult.

## Three tips for representing Christ

FIRST, conduct yourself in a manner compassionate and gracious. Instead of making people caught on the dark side feel like outsiders in our homes or kicking them out of our churches, we set extra places at our dining room tables and cook their favorite meals. We make them welcome. We draw them to us as we are drawn to God. Next, we engage in pleasant conversation, listening carefully and without judgment. Going even further, we lovingly remember birthdays or other occasions that are important to them. These are small, but effective ways to represent God's mercy. Although these techniques might take a little time and effort, they work better toward salvation than hitting occultists over the head with the fact that their practices are going to send them straight to Hell.

SECOND, be calm and loving, but truthful and direct. When occultists confront you with the issues of their belief systems, respond directly and answer truthfully in a calm and loving manner, but don't badger. They might discount everything you say, but they will remember heartfelt truth and the spirit behind loving words long after the conversation has ended. In that same spirit of love, no matter how exasperating the conversations might be, always make yourself available when they need to talk, offer to pray for their needs, ask for forgiveness when you have offended them (and you will), and forgive them freely when they have offended you (and they will).

THIRD, when the time is right, tell them about God. Eventually conversation will open an opportunity to speak openly about the great God who loves us all, no matter how far we have strayed. This is the time to gently "witness." The root of the word "witness" goes back to the Greek word "marturia," "martur," or "martus," interestingly defined as one who gives testimony by his death. Another interpretation is, "one who can or does what he has seen or heard or known." Considered together, the interpretations of "witness" mean that we need to be willing to lay our lives down in testimony of the One whom we've seen, heard and known. What a sobering concept. Suddenly, witnessing is no longer an ice cream social or even telling an unbeliever the story of the Gospel, although these things certainly are included. Witnessing in the biblical sense is the actual laying down our lives so that others may see the compassion, graciousness, mercy, love, faithfulness, and forgiveness of our Lord and Savior Jesus Christ.

Let's turn to some practical application.

## The Occult and Your Child

The first place to start in any family is on your knees before the Lord. Prayer is by far the most effective thing that you can do for your family. There is nothing that can top the effect that a lifetime of prayer will have.

Prevention is worth a pound of cure.

The best time to take a stand against the stronghold of the occult over your family is well before they begin to look at the occult.

Parents, the occult is being marketed to your children at an unprecedented level through movies, television programs, books, games, toys, and trading cards. It's portrayed as innocent, fun, and entertaining. To see the newest or latest in occult items for kids, turn on the television, browse the children's department at the local bookstore, or walk the aisles of the toy store nearest you. The occult is everywhere, and you need to be informed and prepared. The next time you go shopping, take a small pad of paper and jot down items related to the occult that are aimed at your child. This way you'll have a personal understanding and an alarming grasp of the scope of quiet, relentless saturation.

Don't make the mistake of underestimating the power of peer pressure. All kids have access to the occult; many kids dabble in it in some form. Your child is going to be exposed to it in a way that suggests that it's all right. After all, it's everywhere. It's up to you to teach your child that just because the occult is pervasive and familiar, it doesn't make it right. In fact, this pervasive familiarity is sinister. Because our children are being desensitized to the actual, evil reality by this onslaught of occultic imaging, they accept it as a normal, harmless part of life. Kids will even question our wisdom when we attempt to correct their perceptions. From a very early age, this constant occultic barrage will breed a worldview that's blatantly anti-Christian. Even while parents are rearing their kids in churches and in Christian families, the occult is creeping in everywhere.

Once a Christian parent realizes just how much there is out there, the typical response is to overreact and start taking away games and books. The television is turned off. Music is silenced. The computer gets locked in the den. Parental instinct is to protect and shield children from harm and evil influence. But trying to hermetically seal your kids off from the world might not be the best way to defend Christian boundaries against the occult.

You might be able to create a godly environment at home, but you will not be able to protect your children once they walk out the front door. The world is rife with occultism. Because of the saturation of the occult in our society, it's going to be impossible to keep your children away from everything ... and keep everything away from your children.

## The best defense is a good offense

Take an active role in teaching your children and be involved in their lives. Your children are significantly influenced by other children, but are most influenced by you. Start by going to the "Harry Potter" movie with your children. Be silent during the movie. Rest assured there is no demon that's going to come on you, or oppress you just because you went. Once you have the information you need, discuss the movie together over ice cream. You will be able to gently instill your point of view. At the same time, you can begin to teach your child to make distinctions between reality and fantasy, truth and lies, right and wrong, and godly and ungodly. Being able to make a distinction is the first step in being able to make an informed decision. You'll begin to give your child the rudimentary tools for sorting out good and evil.

A good example of the need for your child to make distinctions between good and evil, and fantasy and reality is "Harry Potter." This story of a young boy who studies wizardry in a magical boarding school is a multi-million dollar, multi-national marketing phenomenon, complete with books, movies, toys, and clothes. Few can deny that Harry Potter is a charming tale, but it gives children an unrealistic perspective of the use of magick. Today your child might be mesmerized by enchantment in a movie. Tomorrow, he'll be purchasing the "The

Teen Witch Book," and getting very serious about sorcery. How can you stop this progression and still allow your child to join the other children as they all experience Harry Potter? Simple. Read it together, and discuss as you go along. Help your child to reason things through. Before you know it, your child will be able to distinguish between things that are appropriate and true in Christ ... and those that are not.

Proverbs 6:22 says: "Train a child in the way he should go, and when he is old he will not turn from it." In the context of this Scripture, the word "train" means to discipline a child through education in the direction he is to go.

As a parent, training your children is your primary responsibility and great privilege. It is through educating them that you teach and lead them to make decisions for themselves. When they have been taught and shown truth, they know truth, and will begin to base their decisions on it. However, making good decisions is still up to them. Just as no one could force you into Christianity, you cannot force your child to be a Christian either. He must decide to follow Jesus on his own. You can't force, but you can "train" and lead.

## Listen to your child

I had several spiritual experiences during my childhood because of my innocent involvement in occultic practices: the Ouija board and an out-of-body experience. Having an adult to help and pray with me would have made a world of difference in my ability to withstand the assault of Satan in my life. Your child needs to know that your door is always open and you listen. In other words, if your child comes to you and says that there is a bad person or something bad is happening in his bedroom, he needs to know that you're going to take that (seemingly absurd) declaration very seriously, and further, he can count on you to go immediately into the room to pray for it ... and him. Even if you think that nothing demonic is going on, your child needs to see that it's important to you because it's important to him, and you don't hesitate to respond. Pray a prayer welcoming the Lord Jesus Christ to watch over your child while he sleeps and is alone in his room. Here is a prayer that you might want to pray with your child:

> "Lord Jesus, we love You and welcome You to this bedroom. We ask, Lord, that you live here and watch over (child's name) as he plays and sleeps here. We thank you that (the bad experience) will not happen again, because you are here now, and You are protecting (child's name). In Jesus' name, Amen."

The purpose of this prayer is twofold. First, it's a prayer for protection for your child. Second and equally important is that your child sees your involvement, and witnesses the power of an appropriate prayer for inviting Jesus Christ to be Lord of any situation in his life.

Parents, if your child has a bad spiritual experience with ghosts, monsters, bad dreams etc., you might need to go into his room when he's not there, and take spiritual authority over the activity. Satan may be attempting to cause fear, a tormenting experience or even an enticing one while you are not around.

> "Lord Jesus Christ, we thank You that You defeated Satan when You died on the cross and rose again. We ask that You be the Lord of this home and of this room. We dedicate our lives, family and home to You. Please live here with

us. We take authority, in the name of Jesus Christ, over (name the activity) and command the activity to cease and leave. And, Jesus, we thank You for the victory over this through Your Blood. Amen."

Another thing you can do to keep your child safe is to start a library of *good* children's literature. Make a practice of reading to your child before bedtime. I recommend: "Veggie Tales," "Curious George," "Peanuts," anything from the "Little House on the Prairie" and "Little Women" series, and books about heroes such as Abraham Lincoln or Robin Hood. It's also imperative that children have age-appropriate Bibles that you read together and Christian music to which the whole family listens.

The last thing I would like to suggest is a weekly family night to celebrate your family. Fill it full of favorite food, games, and movies, and end it with family prayer, and prayer requests from your kids. If this is a joyful tradition in your family, even when your kids are older and start establishing independence, you'll be able to count on one night a week when they'll want to be home.

### The occult in middle school

Middle school years are the years that your child will become very socially conscious. It is a time when he'll pull away from you and align himself with other kids. Suddenly you'll think you don't know this child at all. Even when this happens, I urge you to always stay connected. At a time when this becomes difficult, it's more important than ever to set special time aside to be with your child, and to attend school functions.

Father, your role in your son's life is imperative. No one can teach your son to be a Christian man better than you. It's your job to show him how. If you're an ever-present father, he can watch and learn from you. Talk to him ... man to man. Put your arm around him. Explain why you treat your wife the way you do, so that he in turn will develop godly respect for women. By your good example, teach him what it is to be a loving father.

Father, your role in your daughter's life is imperative. Set aside special time each week to be alone with her. In middle school, a little girl grows into womanhood. It's a difficult transition that goes more smoothly when she's sure she's beautiful and loved without question. No one can instill this better than you. During your special time together, treat her like a Christian and a lady. Open the car door for her. Show her the same kind of respect that you will want her future husband to show her.

Mother, your role in your son's life is imperative. No one can better demonstrate the strength and grace of women than you can. It's your job to teach your son to respect and love women, and to use your relationship with his father to teach him how to be a good partner in a balanced relationship. It's also your role to love unconditionally in a relationship of acceptance and nurturing. No one can bring tenderness and sweetness to a young man's life like his mother.

Mother, your role in your daughter's life is imperative. She will learn how to be a Christian woman through your example. You're the one in the family who knows exactly how her body is changing and how she's growing up. Keep the lines of communication open so that she can come to you with anything, and will seek your counsel on all her decisions. Eventually her roles as a Christian professional woman, wife and mother will be modeled from all that she's learned through observing you.

During the middle school years, your child will be facing the world in a much more real way. Be aware of personal issues. Is your child prone to anger or depression? Does she have a healthy self-esteem? Is he fitting in socially at school and in other places? This is a time of changes, fears and anxieties. Think back in your own life. What were you like during the 6th, 7th and 8th grades? What were you like around your parents? What were you like around your friends? How were those two sets of relationships different? Exactly how much did your parents know about what went on at school and during free time with your buddies? Don't be suspicious; be prepared.

A good social place for middle school kids is a GOOD Bible-based youth group. You might at this point start trying to turn them on to the latest in Christian magazines and music. Wonderful magazines are "Brio" for girls and "Breakaway" for boys. Keep your car radio tuned to a good Christian station. Music is very important at this age, and it's possible to help your children develop a taste for Christian music. Encourage them to accompany their youth group to Christian concerts. Purchase CDs and posters of favorite musicians.

Middle school is also a time when kids are hit even harder with occult marketing. Occult-themed movies and television like "Buffy" and "Charmed" are aimed at their particular demographic. Additionally and significantly, the number of books marketed to middle school girls increases dramatically. I call your attention to *The Teen Witch* by Ravenwolf, a practical "how to" that claims help in areas from social status to homework, and "how the occult could work for you." Also there is

*The Daughters of the Moon* series that features four young ladies: Vanessa, who can turn invisible; Kathy, who travels in time; Serena, who has the ability to read minds; and Jimena, who has premonitions. Then there is the Cirque Du Freak series, which describes itself as "a perfect book for reluctant middle school readers. For those fans of Buffy, and Angel, here is another book to satisfy their vampiric tastes." All these books help create dissatisfaction with normal everyday life, and depict a very exciting life revolving around the occult.

If you discover your child reading a book with an occultic theme, don't snatch it away. You'll either create a power struggle or drive your child into secrecy. He's going to read the book whether you like it or not. After all, your banning a book turns it into "forbidden fruit," and nothing is more compelling than that. The better way to handle this is for you to read it, too, and then discuss it. It will be a wonderful opportunity for teaching your child to discern good from evil. The good news is that the presence of a book doesn't cause a demon to enter a Christian home; the demon must be invited. So although your child might not yet be properly trained in discernment, he is in little danger. Through open communication and careful teaching, you can make sure that the invitation is never issued, even inadvertently.

Replace inappropriate books with good ones: C. S. Lewis's *The Chronicles of Narnia*, Madeleine L'Engle's *A Wrinkle in Time*, Walter Farley's *The Black Stallion*, and Rhoald Dahl's *Charlie and the Chocolate Factory*.

If you discover your child dabbling in the occult at any level, remain calm. Likely that she is simply testing the waters. Simply let your child tell you about her interests. Have confidence that you will be able to exert influence sufficient to bring her back in the right direction with logical discussion. Remind her that God has an amazing plan for her life, and that you are so excited to see just what God has in store; God's way is better.

Keep in mind the profound power of prayer. Hold your family in constant prayer as you hold each individual child. There is no more effective weapon available to us against the forces of darkness than prayer.

## The occult in high school

By the time your child reaches high school, social matters dominate their priorities. Now you really must take the time to remember when you were this age. How well did your parents REALLY know you? How much of a secret life did you live? Don't be suspicious; just be prepared. Ready or not, your child is reaching toward independence. This is a very difficult age. Power struggles are normal. When your child was in middle school, you might have been able to get by with, "Do it." But high school aged kids demand detailed explanation worthy of a trial lawyer.

During high school, some teens will "try on" the occult. They might even dabble in different practices, which may or may not lead to more serious involvement. Angry teens tend to be drawn into the darker occultic practices such as Satanism and Witchcraft. Depressed teens are drawn into the Gothic scene. The occult appears to offer answers to the teen who questions, acceptance to the misfit, and power to the powerless.

Teens try to develop an individual sense of spirituality. They no longer want to believe mindlessly what you do. They want to own what they believe. It's very important for Christianity to be real for these teens, because by the age of 18, eighty percent of people who accept Jesus as Lord and Savior have already done so.

Be aware of the music to which your teen is listening, and the movies and television he's watching. Be involved. Discuss everything. Be acutely aware of your role as a Christian. Be humble, honest, and quick to ask for and grant forgiveness. You're being watched.

If you find that despite everything, your teen is involved in the occult, make it your business to know exactly what's going on. Resist the urge to overpower your child. A direct confrontation at this point will do little more than shut down communications between you. Besides, you have homework to do first. Instead of rushing to Christian books on the subject, read the books he's reading and visit the related websites and chat rooms. Wherever your child goes for information and support, be there. Explore the subject completely and quickly. Then and only then you will be able to enter into an intelligent, calm conversation.

When you approach the subject with your teen, three things must be clear. First, you love him unconditionally. Second, you respect him. But don't allow him to mistake love and respect for endorsement, which brings us to the third clear point: although his practice is unacceptable, you forgive him. Your conversation and manner must be Christ-like in gentleness and authority: lots of listening and godly teaching based on all you hear.

Practically speaking, of course, you must draw some lines. For example: "I'm aware that you believe differently; however, we would still need for you to go to church with us as a family on Sunday. And we would like for you to continue attending youth group." Keep a close, but unobtrusive tab on his friends. Be completely aware of comings and goings: who, what, when, where, why, and how. Stay in touch with parents of his friends. We would suggest that you even concoct an excuse and just "pop in" on your teen, particularly if he's spending the night away from your home. If you observe that the draw of the occult is clouding his judgment and leading him away from you, tighten up restrictions.

Make sure that you let your Youth Pastor know that the occult has reared its ugly head. Count on him to be your partner in helping to affix Christ in your child's life, but don't completely trust that responsibility to him. We suggest that you attend their meetings on occasion to make sure your teen is in attendance and that the Youth Pastor is passionate and effective in working for your teen's salvation. Monitor your teen's Sunday school class with the same dogged determination. You might want to encourage your youth program to purchase a quarterly subscription to "For Youth Leaders Only" by Interl'inc. It contains the newest and best of Christian music, Bible studies and videos. What a wonderful resource!

In addition, add a quiet Christian spin to your teen's activities. If sports are his passion, simply subscribe to a Christian sports magazine and leave it lying around. If music is his passion, choose a Christian music magazine and invest in a few really good CDs. If you're unsure about what to buy, many Christian book and music stores make it easy for you to listen to the CD before you choose. Or if you're unable to preview a CD, you can purchase samplers: CDs with songs by different artists. You can hardly go wrong. The point is to subliminally introduce the concept that Christianity isn't an entity unto itself; it's the plan that God has for us …

your teen included. Soon he'll get the idea that it's entirely possible to enjoy all the good things in life, and still be godly. In fact, life's better that way.

A good place for information is the "Focus on the Family" web site. I recommend their publication, "Plugged-In," which is aimed toward parents. It has very good information on what is happening in current youth culture.

I strongly suggest that you institute a weekly family night. Pick one night a week when everyone is at home. Make it a celebration of favorite foods, laughter, games, and movies. Always end the evening with prayer. Pray individually over each child; have your children pray for each other and for you.

Speaking of prayer, if you haven't been praying over your family all along, start NOW. Right now. I'm not talking about dinner time prayer, although this, too, is important. I mean that you need to take your family before the Lord on a daily basis. Praying IS the most important thing a parent can do.

# Chapter Eighteen

# Reaching the Lost

**THIS SECTION IS FOR RESCUING** adult friends, coworkers, and family members who have chosen the trap of the occult. Here's what to do when you find out that the friend you grew up with is a Witch, or the person at the computer next to you is a Druid, or your cousin has been playing with a Ouija board.

Instead of locking yourself away from these people, see the disclosure of occult practices as a wonderful, blessed opportunity for witnessing. Our experiences at Refuge Ministries have taught us much about dealing with adults in the occult. First, remember that adults have probably well thought out their decisions to turn away from Christianity and turn toward occultism. Second, keep in mind that most people like to be "right," so any challenge to their decisions is seen as an indictment. Defenses go up; discussions shut down. So here are a few tips for establishing a conversation:

1. Come in peace.

2. Show respect.

3. Listen.

4. Listen.

5. Listen.

6. Live your witness. As St. Frances of Assisi wisely said, " Preach the Gospel always. If necessary, use words."

7. Realize that your actions speak louder than words, and you're being watched, so act in honesty and humility, strength and gentleness.

Once a mutually respectful relationship has been established, the occultist will begin to see the truth of Christ in you. Remember, everyone—from the Neo-Pagan to the Satanist—is on a spiritual journey to seek **truth**. When you live the truth in front of them, they are drawn toward it.

Among non-Christians, there are a lot of misconceptions about who God is and who He is not. We need to remember the example set by Paul when he was in Athens. Paul approached the Greeks with dignity and respect. He recognized that they worshiped quite a few gods. So, he introduced them very respectfully to "The Unknown God."

> *Then Paul stood in the midst of the Aeropagus and said, "Men of Athens, I perceive that in all things you are very religious; for as I was passing through and considering the objects of your worship, I even found an alter with this inscription; TO THE UNKNOWN GOD. Therefore, the One whom you worship without knowing, Him I proclaim to you"* *(Acts 17:22-23 NKJV).*

As an aside, it does you no good to remind a Satanist that he is going to hell. That's what he WANTS! To a Satanist, hell is a reward.

When the opportunity finally arises, and you are able to discuss beliefs, we have a good technique for you. Ask questions. Don't make statements. For example, instead of saying "Witches are talking to demons when they think that they are talking to the dead," you might say something like, "I understand that some Witches talk to the spirits of dead people. How can you be sure that the spirit is who he says he is?" Then you can gently let them know that the Bible tells *us* not to believe every spirit, but to test the spirits to see if they are from God (1 John 4:1). Then you can ask, "Do you have a way that you can test a spirit?" Once you can get people to THINK, they'll almost lead themselves to Christ. But just in case the discussion becomes specific, make sure you know your own faith as well as they do theirs. If you stumble and falter, they'll know for sure that you don't know what you're talking about, and conversation will terminate. Credibility is a key factor in leading an occultist to the Lord. If you don't have an answer, you can ask for time to research. There's nothing wrong in, "May I get back to you on that one? I want to make sure I'm giving you the accurate information you deserve." Or you can simply ask the Lord to take over. Quiet yourself and pray for guidance: "Lord, what will You have me say now?"

## The importance of prayer

There's no doubt in my mind that praying is the single most important thing that you can do for other people and yourself. There is nothing more effective than going before the throne of God on the behalf of someone who is lost.

The more you pray, the more exciting it becomes. Prayer connects us to the very heart of God. Get in the habit now. Don't wait to pray until there is nothing left to do but pray. There are many reasons and ways to pray, of course, but when you are praying for someone, this is called an *intercessory prayer.* It is literally your stepping up on someone else's behalf and asking God to bless him or her. The person for whom the prayer is offered doesn't need to know about the prayer. And if he or she knows about it and disapproves, it doesn't matter. Intercessory prayer is between you and God. He listens and answers. I firmly believe that the prayers of my mother and those people who knew me helped me to find the Lord. And to Jeff Harshbarger, the Satanist, finding the Lord was a matter of life and death. So it will be with the occultist you are trying to save. Pray. Pray often. Pray hard. It's a matter of life and death.

So how do you pray? Go to the Lord in prayer for the people for whom you have concern. Seek forgiveness for any offense you have committed. Humbly relinquish your right to know how things should happen in submission to the One who has any REAL rights at all. Your responsibility is to ask God to rescue. The work itself is not your responsibility. The work belongs to God. If you humble yourself through your witness, being sure to lay down your life, you'll be an open channel for God to use. This is a privilege that you should take seriously and honor humbly.

Remember, praying does not put you in charge. When we want something very badly (like rescuing a loved one), we all have a very human tendency to tell God what we want, how we want it done, and when it has to happen. Then we sit back and watch the (soon-to-be former) occultist in breathless anticipation. We're pretty sure that he'll change any minute. This couldn't be more wrong.

No matter how well intentioned, once a Christian tries to manipulate a person, the next step is to manipulate the situation, and to even try to control what and how God operates. This sequence of rebellion is essentially a form of Witchcraft. Believe me, an occultist *will* recognize Christian Witchcraft. He'll leave skid marks trying to get away from the situation. You won't make that mistake. You'll always be mindful of the direct connection between humbling yourself in prayer, relinquishing your right to know, and honoring the privilege of being used by God. In other words, you go before the Father and instead of asking to manipulate the person or circumstance, you simply ask the Lord to open their eyes so that they may be enlightened with the truth of God. This way, they will begin to see God clearly. Once this happens, God is extremely hard to resist.

You might pray something like these:

"Lord God, I actively choose to relinquish my rights to manipulate this situation. Let Your will be done, not mine. I humbly ask that you send me and keep me in tune with You, so that Your will be done. In Jesus name, Amen."

Another good prayer for the people whom you are trying to reach comes right out of the Book of Ephesians:

"God of our Lord Jesus Christ, the glorious Father, may you please give (name) the Spirit of wisdom and revelation so that (name) may know him better. I pray also that the eyes of (name) heart may be enlightened in order that (name) may know the hope to which he has called (name) in the riches of his glorious inheritance in the saints and his incomparably great power for us who believe" (Ephesians 1:17-21).

This is a very powerful prayer to pray over an occultist because:

> "The god of this age has blinded the minds of unbelievers, so that they cannot see the light of the gospel of the glory of Christ, who is the image of God" (2 Corinthians 4:4).

Keep in mind that although you can ask God to intervene, you cannot interfere with the free will of an individual. Even with our responsibility to pray and God's willingness to save, people do have the right to choose death. When they choose this path, there is nothing you can do. This is one of the saddest truths that I know. That being said, NEVER give up the fight, but daily lay your life down for the lost, and trust the One who can save them from death. It's our responsibility to be lights in their darkness.

In closing this section of the book, I would like to share with you a letter from Annie Fintan. Annie, as you will read about her in the next chapter, was deeply involved in the darker side of European Witchcraft. She has come to a saving knowledge of the Lord Jesus Christ, and it's her now calling to help others who have taken the same path that she had.

When I asked what advice she gives to those who have someone they care about involved in the occult, she said:

"First of all, don't 'go after them,' and try to show them where they are wrong. You don't want it to be an 'I'm right, you're wrong' situation. There is a reason that they believe what they do, and we need to respect that.

"I firmly believe that if you have a close relationship with Christ, then your relationship will show up in your day-to-day living. You may not even notice, but others will. We need to be living examples. We need to be authentic in Christ.

"Those who walk the Left Hand Path are usually incredible judges of character. It's sometimes a dangerous journey, and their life often depends on the ability to spot a fake. You're not perfect, and all of us are human, but don't be a hypocrite.

"For most of my life, I refused to even consider Christianity because of the many hypocrites. I have seen hypocrites of all flavors. Some acted as if they had an interest in me, but really only wanted to make themselves look pious by showing concern. Others sought me out to tell me just how wrong I was for my Pagan beliefs, but yet their own beliefs were shallow at best. There are other examples that I could use, but what I'm saying is, don't act out of pride because you see yourself above those poor Pagans. Many of them put Christians to shame, because they are much more devoted to their constant pursuit of a stronger spirituality than many Christians are to imitating Jesus.

"The only time they will hear us is when we speak out of genuine love and humility. But even before they will hear us, they will be watching our lives to see if we are authentic.

"Prayer is our greatest tool. People have approached me and asked what they can do to reach someone they care about. When I responded, "Pray for them," I have been met with the response, "Oh, is that all?"

"Is that all??? What greater work could we ever do than to carry someone to the throne of Almighty God and intercede on his or her behalf? Through prayer, we get to be a part of the amazing work God wants to do."

# Chapter Nineteen

# Success Stories and a Final Word

THE STORIES IN THIS CHAPTER are those of real people. Those whom God sends to Liz and me more often than not become a part of our family. We know them well and love them deeply. We have been honored to be a part of these stories and many others. We know that God is faithful and is an ever-present help in times of trouble.

## Jo Ana's story

The first time my wife Liz and I saw Jo Ana, we had been enjoying a long stint in full time Youth Ministry and had just arrived in a new church. I can remember walking into the youth room and seeing her in a small group of average looking teenagers, huddled around a table in the collective, typical, half asleep look that clearly says, "I'd rather be in bed on Sunday morning." What I didn't know was that among them, huddled a practicing Wiccan. At first glance, we, like everyone, were deceived into thinking that if she looks like a Christian, acts like a Christian, and attends church like a Christian, then she MUST be a Christian. We were wrong. The evidence was right under our noses. Even her parents were deceived. All they had to do was look around her neck or walk into her bedroom to know that something was very, very wrong.

What Jo Ana's parents didn't know was that she had become friends with the daughter of a Wiccan while she was in middle school. The friend was very well behaved and friendly. She seemed to be the kind of kid that parents would love to have befriend their child. But appearances can be deceiving. Every time Jo Ana went over to play with her friend, she was being trained in Wiccan practices. In a short time, Jo Ana's view of Christianity changed. She now thought that Jesus was just one in a line of prophets, all of whom led to the same place. Before her parents had any idea, she was practicing Wiccan and sharing her new beliefs with her friends at school and at church.

Jo Ana's attitude began to change. She became moody. Her parents attributed it to puberty. Increasingly unhappy with her parents' conservative lifestyle, Jo Ana began to detach from them. When she started high school, she preferred the company of kids who practiced the craft and liked to party. By the time my wife and I had arrived at this church, Jo Ana had been involved in Wicca for some time, and also had been sneaking out of the house and dabbling in drugs, as well.

Liz and I noticed the Wiccan symbol around her neck right away. Liz asked, "Hey, what is that around your neck? Are you into Wicca?" I think that Jo Ana was so surprised and pleased that we knew what she was wearing and that we asked respectfully that she told us without hesitation, "Why, yes, I am!"

In the next year, Liz and I pursued Jo Ana by merely showing her the love of God. We let her mom know what was going on. Thanks to the guidance of the Holy Spirit and the teamwork that we got from her wonderful mother, slowly but surely Jo Ana started to turn back toward God. Eventually Jo Ana gave her heart to Jesus.

The fun part began as we watched the Lord change her completely. Jo Ana stopped hanging out with the drug kids at school, and found that with her new joyful personality, she was suddenly quite popular with everyone else. This young lady became a witnessing machine. She even gave her testimony at school on occasion. Praise God!

## Teresa's story

Teresa came to me through our web site. She had been raised in a Christian family. Her Mom and Dad were prominent members of her church and were there every time the door opened. Teresa, in the middle of her family, was feeling lost, and neither loved nor accepted. She never felt that she quite measured up to her family's high standards. It seemed to her that the harder she worked at chores around the house or the higher her grades at school, the more her family demanded of her. They were perfect, and Teresa should be perfect. She was a very angry and hurt young woman. She started thinking about drinking, smoking or even running away, but the more she thought about it, the more she realized that she wanted to do something a lot more secretive— a quiet form of rebellion that no one would know about but her. One night when Theresa was alone in her bedroom, she decided to pray to Satan. To her surprise, Satan showed up. This scared her so much that she started looking for help, and that's how she found us.

We immediately led her in a prayer of repentance for her prayer to Satan and other sins, and then started to dig for the underlying sources of the hurt and anger that drove her to tap into the dark side. Initially, Teresa didn't know us well enough to trust us completely, and was still seeking help in other places besides us. She ran across a deliverance minister who told her that she had 12 demons. She didn't. He determined her spiritual state by looking into her eyes and "finding" the demons. One after another, he named off 12 demons to this teenaged girl, including a demon of "sleep." Poor Teresa was afraid to go to bed at night. Yes, she was sleepy, but not because of any demon. She had lost so much sleep because of her anxiety-provoking family situation. Thanks to the inexcusable claims of this "ministry," Teresa had even more to deal with than just her family issues.

However, God's grace is sufficient. Eventually, she allowed us to work with her, and together we explored the problems that stemmed not from demons, but from being a little girl growing up in a demanding family. When she learned how to forgive them and herself, Teresa started to shine. She now walks with the Lord, and has attended college. She currently works in a therapeutic capacity with teenagers. Teresa is indeed a testimony to the faithfulness of the Lord.

## Annie Fintan's story

Annie Fintan has had a remarkable journey. Annie wrote her own story, and so we've included it. We hope her story blesses you.

"From the time I was very young, I felt that I was different from the other kids that I knew. I was incredibly sensitive to things of a spiritual nature. Without having an explanation, I often knew things that I had no natural way of knowing. I knew there was a spirit realm, because I had seen spirits. Since I knew of their presence, it seemed only natural to seek what I could learn from them.

"I grew up hearing Christianity presented in many forms, but none of it ever sank past the surface. I heard the teachings of how Jesus was God's Son and that He had died for our sins so that we could one day live in heaven with Him. I knew the hymns, and even memorized a few Scripture verses. However, none of it was real to me. I watched the lives of those Christians who taught of a Savior, and they seemed empty and shallow.

"In my early teens, I left any consideration of Christianity behind, and began searching for truth elsewhere.

"I committed myself to learning all that I could of the spirit realm. Years were spent exploring several different belief systems, but never embraced a particular one. I was quite eclectic in my practices, but was never very humble in my opinions.

"My outspokenness eventually caught the attention of a woman who had years of experience in the occult. She followed a European Tradition, and I was immediately impressed with the position and power that she had. The opinions I expressed seemed to interest her, and she respected my boldness. After spending a lot of time getting to know each other, she offered to assist me in my spiritual search.

"Within a matter of months, I traveled to the UK to meet other members of a European coven. I was impressed with what I found, and eager to learn what I could from them. There was a darker side to this tradition that appealed to me. It offered a sense of power and mystery that I craved.

"My journey eventually led me to Ireland, and when I set foot on the Emerald Isle, I immediately felt as if I had come home. I loved everything about the place. In the Celtic beliefs, I found a spirituality that made sense to me. I was still influenced by aspects of what I had learned in the UK, but primarily I became a Celtic Pagan. The tradition that I learned had been passed down through generations, too secretive to ever be written down. I met many different gods and goddesses, and sought their assistance in my journey. Truth and knowledge were my pursuit.

"I traveled back and forth between Ireland, the UK, and the United States for the next couple of years. I was relentless in my pursuit, always attempting to gain a little bit more knowledge, power, and position. The rest of my life became secondary to my search.

"However, I eventually began to realize that I wasn't finding fulfillment. That little bit more was always just out of reach. I knew that something was going to have to change in my life, but was at a loss when it came to figuring out what I needed. I was prepared to take my own life, rather than meet failure.

"While I was back in the States, an old acquaintance introduced me to some of her friends. I knew from the moment that I laid eyes on them that there was something different about them. I could sense that something within them made that difference, and it raised my curiosity. These people were Christians, but unlike any others I had ever met. They invited me to their home for dinner, and that was the beginning of a whole new world for me. They offered me friendship and love, and as our relationship grew I watched their lives closely. Without any grandeur, they possessed a spirituality that I admired. I began to learn everything I could from them, looking for the source of their peace.

"The following months were a very confusing time for me, trying to maintain my own relationship with the entities I served, while interested in the claims of another God. Unconsciously, I was trying to live with a foot in both worlds.

"It was around that time that I stumbled across Jeff Harshbarger's testimony. His claim of being set free from Satanism drew my attention, and I contacted Refuge Ministries. Jeff and I began to talk, and I immediately recognized a difference in him as well.

"I was thrilled to have found someone who knew the world in which I was involved, someone who had actually been there himself. Gradually, I began sharing my dilemma with him, and began asking my questions. He and his wife offered support and friendship during a time when I felt that no one could possibly understand my pain. Their unconditional love saved my life.

"Stepping back from day to day activities, I took some time to analyze my life. I had traveled the world, gained power and respect, but couldn't find peace. I wrestled with uncertainty for quite some time, walking a razor thin edge between hope and despair.

"I was drawn by the idea of a God of love, a God above all other "gods." I began to urgently study the Bible, wanting to know as much as possible. The more I sought after His Truth, the more it became clear to me that this was what I had been looking for all along.

"After carefully considering the matter, I made the decision to completely commit my life to Christ. The months that followed were filled with a whirlwind of changes. Daily my relationship with God grew stronger, and I found the freedom that He alone could offer.

"The years I spent following the left hand path are a constant reminder to me that there are others searching for the same things I did. God has gently filled me with the desire to share with them what I have found. Just like those who took the time to provide me with the help I needed, I want to make myself available to help others in any way I can.

"Jeff and Liz helped make that possible by inviting me to become a staff member at Refuge Ministries. Together, we instruct others about the dangers of the occult, and other forms of Paganism. God used Refuge Ministries to change my life, and I know He is using it to change the lives of others."

These "success" stories are condensed versions of individual testimonies. Please don't read them and think that it is simple or easy to walk away from involvement in the occult. Deliverance is a process. It takes more than a simple prayer or easy answers. The people in these stories received counsel and were discipled, but still had some rough times. However, each one is walking today with the Lord Jesus Christ.

# A Final Word

**REFUGE MINISTRIES** was born out of need. Over the years, we've met many people who have loved ones involved in the occult or who were involved themselves. They were all looking for the same thing: a ministry that would touch them gently and take their need seriously without making them feel like outcasts. We had been helped so much through Jo and Harry Richardson. Every time we would try to thank them, Jo would say, "The best way that you can thank us is to turn around and help others in the same way that we helped you." It's hard to ignore words like those.

I can remember marveling to Jo one afternoon about how much she must know in regard to deliverance and counseling. Jo laughed and said, "Really, I never knew what I was doing! I just prayed real hard and tried to listen to the Lord." As Jo taught me, I hope I've taught you: You don't have to know what you're doing, and God can still use you.

So, when people ask us how we do what we do, we'll always say that the base of our ministry is love and re-parenting. When the Lord sends people our way, we try to be the parents they always wished they had. We are very tough, but loving. We know that God does all the work, and we have the privilege of serving God as He performs miracles.

If, after all that you have been through, you find that you still need some help, it would be our honor to help you. We are available for seminars, training, and prayer, or anything else you might need. Let me warn you, though. We are tenacious and will hold you accountable, so we ask that you are serious about working with us.

## To contact us:

Refuge Ministries
P. O. Box 1273
Thomson, GA 30824
www.refugministries.cc
or email: info@refugeministries.cc.

I would like to conclude by saying that God is faithful! He will never leave you or forsake you! He does deliver. Your loved one can recover. I'm proof. It's been over two decades since that young man who failed at everything, including suicide, was made whole. What God has done for me, He will do for you.

*"He is our Refuge and Strength, a very present help in trouble" (Psalm 46:1).*